Sharing the
Kingdom

Animals and Their Rights

Sharing the Kingdom

Animals and Their Rights

Karen O'Connor

Illustrated with photographs

DODD, MEAD & COMPANY

New York

For my colleague and dear friend
Gray Johnson Poole

Acknowledgments

My sincere appreciation to all of the individuals and organizations whose friendly cooperation and assistance with interviews, photographs, and printed materials contributed to the writing of this book.

Photograph Credits

American Fund for Alternatives to Animal Research (AFAAR), 116, 117; American Humane Association, 16, 40; The Animal Care and Education Center, 8, 23, 26; Animal Welfare Institute, 76; Associated Press Photo courtesy of The American Horse Protection Association, 82; Beauty Without Cruelty, 95; R. A. Brown, FACT, Inc., 59, 62; John J. Dommers, The Humane Society of the United States, 123; Edmonton Journal, 111; Courtesy of Gwen Hutchinson, 36; J. A. Keller, Animal Rights Network, 15, 56, 57, 60, 68, 70; Chuck Kneyse, IDAHO STATESMAN, courtesy of The American Horse Protection Association, 80; Courtesy of Marlene Lakin, 125; Monterey County Society for the Prevention of Cruelty to Animals, 85; Karen O'Connor, 24, 83, 87, 96, 108; Peninsula Humane Society, 122; PETA, 91, 92; Kelle Rankin, 11; Courtesy of the San Diego County Humane Society, 19, 20, 38 (by Bert Shanklund); Courtesy of Laura Simon, 124; SIO Photo, 101, 102; UCSD, 106; Union-Tribune Publishing Co., 32, 49, 64; Wide World Photos, 34; © Zoological Society of San Diego, 43.

1   2   3   4   5   6   7   8   9   10

Library of Congress Cataloging in Publication Data

O'Connor, Karen.
  Sharing the kingdom.

  Bibliography: p.
  Includes index.
  Summary: Examines the issue of animal rights
discussing the use of animals in laboratory experiments,
factory farms, and in entertainment.
  1. Animals, Treatment of—United States—Juvenile
literature. [1. Animals—Treatment] I. Title.
HV4764.038 1984   179'.3   84-10329
ISBN 0-396-08460-5

Contents

"Animals are such agreeable friends—they ask no questions, they pass no criticisms."

—George Eliot

". . . money . . . is really the difference between men and animals; most of the things men feel animals feel and vice versa, but animals do not know about money; money is purely a human conception and that is very important to know, very very important."

—Gertrude Stein

Many dogs await adoption.

Chapter One
What Are Animal Rights, Anyway?

It was the week before Christmas, and Mrs. Bates thought it would be nice if she went down to her local shelter and groomed the dogs so they might have a better chance of being adopted. When she arrived at the Hardin County (Ohio) dog pound, she found the waiting room "packed full" of people waiting for adoption hours to start. Many had seen ads in the local paper the day before and had already picked out the animals they wanted.

But the prospective pet owners went home that day both disappointed and horrified. While they sat and waited for the arrival of the dog warden, another visitor had come and gone. The visitor was a local "buncher" [someone who rounds up pets at the pound and then sells them to laboratories], who operated under an agreement with the pound. This man came in, took all the dogs he thought he could resell to research laboratories, and euthanized [killed] the rest. "When he left," said Mrs. Bates, "all that was left was a couple of coon dog puppies. But before he got there, there were enough adopters to have given homes to all the animals."

Mrs. Bates' story as reported in *Close-up*, the official publication of The Humane Society of the United States, is not new. Domestic pets are used for medical research in almost every state in the country, even in California, New York, Pennsylvania, Maine, Montana, and others where this practice is clearly against the law.

After I first read this story I began to think about all the pets we had loved and cared for in our family—three dogs, a cat, a parakeet, a hamster, and a horse—and how I might feel if any of them had been lost or stolen and then turned over to a laboratory.

Family pets, however, are not the only animals that suffer even though there are laws to protect them. For example, it is also against the law for carriage and riding horses to be overworked and underfed. Mayor Koch of New York signed such a law in August, 1981. It requires working horses in that city to wear licenses costing $25 a year and take leaves when sick.

Riding horses are not allowed to work more than eight hours in any twenty-four, and carriage horses ten hours out of twenty. When the licenses are renewed, the animals will have to be inspected first. A veterinarian's certificate of good health will be required.

At first most owners obeyed the new law. But within months several drivers were forced to shut down their carriage rides because they had abused and overworked their horses.

IT TAKES MORE THAN A LAW

In most states it is also against the law to abandon a pet, yet people do this every day without thinking much about it. I had a neighbor who left her cat on its own after she and her family moved to another state. She told her children the cat would find its food in the wild. And yet the animal had been a family pet, totally unacquainted with life in the "wild," since its birth.

Perhaps the saddest part of this story is that these are good family people. They care about each other and live in harmony with their neighbors. They could easily live down the street from any one of us. But they are unknowing or just don't care when it comes to taking responsibility for the pets they chose. They act on their feelings or do what's convenient. After all, the cat didn't ask to move in with them. They chose her.

When the family's circumstances changed, the woman made a decision based on what she "thought" would happen, instead of thinking it through, asking for help from a professional, or offering the cat to another family.

Laws, whether for humans or nonhumans, are made in order to protect the rights of people and animals. But they don't mean much unless we believe in what they stand for and are also willing to see that they are enforced.

Slavery, for example, continued in our country for over a hundred years because so many people were unwilling to see it as a violation of human rights. The same thing was true of child labor.

Similar practices exist today regarding the rights of animals. People who think of horses as no more than property to be used and abused aren't likely to obey the horse protection law in New York or any place else.

And individuals who have no understanding of the needs of a domestic pet will go on treating it like a product to be discarded when they're finished, rather than a living, breathing creature to be cared for.

A pet needs a lot of care.

BEHIND THE SCENES

Most of us are unaware of the day-to-day life of the many animals that in some way provide the things we expect and often take for granted—food, clothing, medicine, cosmetics, and various forms of entertainment.

And young people seem especially isolated from what goes on behind the scenes. As a child you were probably first introduced to animals through stories and pictures, visits to the zoo, or a day at a marine park. And yet, the grass-grazing cattle, swinging monkeys, or carefree cats and dogs you met in picture books or at the zoo have little in common with the residents of many modern veal and pig farms, science laboratories, or pet pounds where animals are often cruelly treated for no really worthwhile purpose. And perhaps you have arrived at junior or senior high with little more knowledge about what goes on than you had when you first started school.

This is not to say that animal stories or marine parks should be replaced with gruesome scientific reports and graphic photographs. But on the other hand, as a young person learning and forming opinions about life, you have a right to know the truth—that most animals today live under conditions that are anything but pleasant. By leaving out part of the story, adults may inhibit your right to know all of the facts—to decide for yourself how and where you will direct your energy in the world.

For example, Peter Singer, in his landmark book *Animal Liberation*, cites the case of the young son of a Harvard professor of moral development, who at the age of four, refused to eat meat because, he said, "It's bad to kill animals." His father claimed that the child was at the most primitive stage of moral development and therefore unable to tell the difference between justified and unjustified killing. Determined to change his son's mind, he took six months to talk the boy out of his position. The boy appeared to know what was right for him even

12

at age four. But his father sought to impose his own standards on him.

Singer's book and others have triggered people's awareness. As a result, millions of Americans are now concerned about how we treat the animals in our country. People of every age are getting involved in the movement for animal rights—a cause founded on the principles of justice and morality—which views animals as living, feeling creatures with interests of their own and the same capacity for suffering as humans.

RIGHTS COME FROM LIFE ITSELF

According to the Declaration of Independence, our birth rights or "unalienable Rights" to life, liberty, and the pursuit of happiness come from our Creator. They are part of the gift of life.

Most people seem to agree that all life, animals included, comes from that same Creator or source, yet they don't say much, if anything, about an animal's "unalienable rights."

That's not to say that people and animals will live life or pursue happiness in the same way. Certainly our interests and needs are not the same. Animals, for example, "pursue happiness" primarily through instinct. The important point, then, is not that we are different or similar in how we express life. The important point is that we each do have life. And it is life itself that gives each of us—whether human or nonhuman—the right to express ourselves in keeping with our nature.

Those who want proof for this don't have far to go. The answer lies deep within each one of us—if we are willing to look and listen.

TOOLS OR CREATURES

Today, humanitarians generally agree that cruelty to animals occurs when human beings inflict pain and suffering on them.

The various ways in which animals' rights are exploited seem to fall into three main categories: science, profit, and sport, with some overlapping in each. Science and profit, for example, are both involved in experimentation in the multibillion dollar drug industry.

In one laboratory a baby rhesus monkey was photographed gasping following a test for soap toxicity. Rabbits lined up in stocks become the victims of cosmetic tests. The burning substance used in their eyes resulted in severe damage. And gentle, sociable, rats and mice fight for space in crowded cages, while a dog is strapped to a surgery table and left alone for hours without companionship or medication.

Scientists and concerned citizens are now protesting the necessity of making laboratory animals suffer in order to develop and test products that aren't essential for human well-being. Introducing a new line of lipstick, deodorant, or cleansing solution to a market already crowded with similar products seems insensitive and irresponsible when we look at the cost: the health, well-being, and often life itself of an innocent animal.

HOME ON THE RANGE—NO MORE

Most meat-producing animals, particularly those raised on "factory farms," aren't much better off. Profit is certainly a motive here with the high demand for meat and meat products.

More than one million calves, for example, exist in pens so tight they cannot turn around. To exercise their legs they must push them against the slats of the floor. They live alone and in darkness, unable to touch or see any of their peers. The only change in routine is mealtime, consisting of a special liquid formula used to fatten them up for early slaughter.

These young veal calves will never know the freedom of a romp in the countryside, the taste of new grass, or the warmth of the sun streaming down on their backs. They will live in confinement until three months of age, when they'll be killed for their highly prized white meat.

14

Veal calves are raised in confinement.

FUN OR PROFIT?

To many people, horse and dog racing, films, rodeos, and circuses might be considered entertainment or sport. But how many in the audience know what goes on behind the scenes in order to present these shows.

It is not uncommon for rabbits, ducks, horses, elephants, and monkeys to be provoked, prodded, starved, tripped, teased, and often deliberately killed in order for the "show" to go on.

For example, according to the American Humane Association in Hollywood, California, two rabbits and two ducks were deliberately killed during the filming of the CBS western series "The Chisholms." And five horses died during the filming of

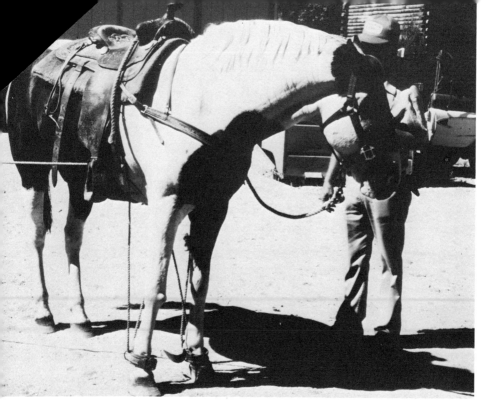

Mock-up of "running W's"

Heaven's Gate because of the use of "running W's" (wire used to force horses to the ground during battle scenes).

AGE-OLD QUESTION

The issue of animal rights is not new. In fact, the relationship between animals and human beings goes back thousands of years. Some civilizations worshiped particular animals. Other cultures believed in animal spirits.

In ancient Greece, Aristotle talked about the differences and similarities between animals and people. "All animals," he wrote, "have one sense at least, and whatever has a sense has the capacity for pleasure and pain . . ." But he also believed that the important difference between animals and humans was that animals do not have intelligence.

The Judeo-Christian view, using the Book of Genesis in the

Bible as its source, says that humankind was made in the image of God and given dominion over animals. Some people use this passage, however, as an excuse to behave as cruel masters instead of firm but gentle stewards.

It was not until the nineteenth century that anyone actually argued *for* an animal's natural rights. Jeremy Bentham, an English jurist-philosopher, claimed that all living creatures should be treated equally. He believed that all *sentient* beings (creatures with feelings) have equal interests. In *The Principles of Morals and Legislation* (1789), he wrote: ". . . A full-grown horse or dog is beyond comparison a more rational, as well as a more conversable animal, than an infant of a day, or a week, or even a month, old. But suppose the case were otherwise, what would it avail? The question is not, Can they reason? nor, Can they talk? but, Can they suffer?"

Anyone who has ever listened to the cries of an electrically shocked beagle or the loud bellowing of a hanging steer before slaughter would have a difficult time denying their ability to suffer.

Today, nearly two hundred years after Bentham's question, many people are beginning to recognize that an animal's capacity for suffering is the fact that must determine how we treat it.

Certainly that does not mean that we should suddenly turn every animal loose to do as they please. As civilization has developed, people and animals have had to learn how to share the planet.

As a result, many of an animal's natural rights have been taken away or at least exchanged for other comforts. For example, pet population control has restricted an animal's right to reproduce. Their need to wander freely is now limited for public safety and their own well-being by specially designated animal parks and wilderness areas. And their need to bark or howl or root up the landscape must be curtailed in neighborhoods where there are families and homes. And of course, like people, not all animals have the same needs. But certain basic rights come with the gift of life itself—humane treatment and the opportunity to experience what is called *telos*—the basic nature of its species, whether it's rooting in the mud, sharpening its claws, or preening in the sun.

"Because we have deprived our pets of so many of their natural rights," says Dr. Michael Fox, director of the Institute for the Study of Animal Problems in Washington, D.C., "we must take special care to preserve those that they can still enjoy—the right to play and affection, exercise, training, medical care, a balanced diet, and, when the time eventually comes, to a humane death."

FACTS WE DON'T WANT TO FACE

There is still much work to be done in educating and alerting the public to the pain, suffering, and outright cruelty that is inflicted on millions of animals each year in the laboratories, schools, homes, and farms of our country. And since the animals involved cannot speak for themselves, it is up to us to speak for them.

Of course, there are some people who are not ready to hear the facts. Those busy nibbling a fried chicken wing or barbecuing a hamburger, for example, may not be interested in how that meal got to their plates. And when a new line of facial products appears on the cosmetic counter, we're not particularly anxious to learn how many rabbits lost their eyes or their lives in order to test the products' safety.

In the face of such unpleasant facts, it's a lot more comfortable to regard the rights of animals and those who support them as a crusade headed up by emotion-charged pet lovers.

"Loving" animals, however, has nothing to do with the purpose of the animal rights movement. It's not some weekend hobby or classroom project for dog lovers. People who feel strongly about the rights of animals see this cause as an impor-

Dog groomer Betty B of Betty B's Poodle Salon in San Diego with a few happy customers

Love at first sight!

tant moral movement, founded on the principles of justice, every bit as urgent as the issue of abortion or rape today, or slavery and women's right to vote were in their time.

Today, as we become more aware of the quality of our own lives through natural foods, yoga, meditation, exercise, weight control, clean air and so on, we need to ask ourselves whether or not we can continue to stand by and watch animals be denied their same right to life, in keeping with their nature and interests.

There are many questions to be answered, and many problems to be solved—none easy. But no answers will ever be discovered unless each of us takes the first steps—facing the problems, learning as much as we can, participating in the area where we can be the most useful, and then drawing our own conclusions. I hope the information in the following chapters will help you take those first steps.

Chapter Two
How We Treat Man's Best Friend

Did you know that every hour ten thousand kittens and puppies are born in the United States—most of them unwanted? That millions more roam the streets? And that 18 to 25 million are "put to sleep" each year in local pounds and shelters? The cost to the public is another staggering figure—up to $30 apiece to process each animal. This involves capturing, feeding, and eventually killing them.

The Society for Animal Rights (SAR) claims that the suffering of unwanted dogs and cats is a subject that has had too little attention. As more and more unwanted animals pour into pounds and shelters day after day, the need for mass killing continues. And in the process, the real work of humane societies—to prevent cruelty and suffering—must be set aside as workers are needed to carry out mass euthanasia (mercy killing) programs.

"The need for killing can be steadily and dramatically reduced," however, according to Helen Jones, president of SAR. A few areas are now using a three-part plan that seems to work well. It includes: (1) spay/neuter clinics, (2) public information and law enforcement, and (3) shelter operation.

The Humane Society of Lackawanna County in Pennsylvania, in conjunction with the Society of Animal Rights, is now putting such a plan into operation. They are building a new shelter that will include a full-time spay/neuter clinic, an educational unit to provide the community with information about all kinds of animals and their needs, and a modern shelter designed to keep the animals comfortable.

Each dog will have a double run to make cleaning easier and more efficient. Special quarters will be designed for puppies and kittens. And cats will not only have cages, but also an exercise/play area. One room will be used for interviewing people who wish to adopt animals. And there will also be an area where animals and adopters can have time to get acquainted.

"Our goal," said Mrs. Jones, in a letter to SAR members, "is to bring about a steady reduction in the numbers of animals reaching the shelter as unwanted and homeless. That will be achieved through the spay/neuter clinic and a dynamic public information and education campaign."

SAR and the Humane Society intend that this new shelter serve as "a national model of what can be done to prevent the tragedy of homeless, unwanted animals."

Meanwhile, on the opposite coast, there exists another organization dedicated to educating the community about animal life—The Animal Care and Education Center in Rancho Santa Fe (San Diego County), California. The staff of this unique facility shares with teachers, parents, and schools an interest in humane education.

Incorporated in 1972 as a charitable nonprofit corporation, the Center is dedicated to improving human/animal relationships. For several years it has developed materials and programs to help educate the public toward a humane philosophy and reverence for all living things.

22

Dr. Alice De Groot caring for one of the many "wild" visitors at The Animal Care and Education Center.

Although similar in purpose to a humane society, the Center does not get involved in animal control, cruelty investigation, licensing, or policing. And while humane societies do offer some educational programs, the Center goes into greater depth in this area and provides a wider range of programs and materials.

This ultramodern facility includes the most advanced techniques in animal care in the nation. Kennels were specially designed to promote disease control. Individual runs and radiant-heated floors provide comfort and safety for all the animals. The Center also provides a warm and friendly environment for

Director of Education Ivan Golakoff

bringing animals and people together. And its many unique educational programs have drawn international attention.

SHARING THE EARTH

One such program, *Sharing the Earth*, was recently developed in conjunction with the state of California. This unique packet of classroom materials "met a real need not in existence," said Director of Education Ivan Golakoff. Mr. Golakoff developed the program with Sherri M. Butterfield to meet state requirements that humane education be taught in all public schools.

Geared mainly for the fifth grade level, the one-year project was distributed to all schools in California. However, within the next year or so, they hope to make it available to schools nationwide.

In a letter to educators, the Center's Executive Director Mel Morse talked about the animal suffering they see on a daily basis—"The result of ignorance and misunderstanding—animals, often much-loved family pets, suffering from neglect, improper care, abuse and general irresponsibility; wild animals 'lovingly' removed from their natural habitat, then rejected for their inability to cope in a domesticated environment. The plight of the many abused, unwanted or uncared for animals is a tragedy that reflects on all of us."

Mr. Morse felt that a list of reminders or rules was not enough. "These are meaningless unless placed within a broader understanding of the earth as a community shared by all living things."

Sharing the Earth, stated Mr. Morse, is intended to be a "valuable tool for increasing students' awareness of the world they share with others around them, while expanding their understanding of true caring and compassion for those who are suffering or less fortunate."

THE CENTER AND ANIMAL RIGHTS

When I asked Mr. Golakoff about the Center's involvement with the animal rights movement, he said that they are involved, but in a more subtle way than some other groups. "We are not actively campaigning or protesting, but we are educating the public. We support, in principle, what these groups do but we simply approach it from a different point of view—that of education."

For example, in addition to the classroom program, the Center also sponsors animal programs for the handicapped (therapeutic horseback riding); Pet Encounter Therapy, which includes animal visits to mental health facilities and convalescent

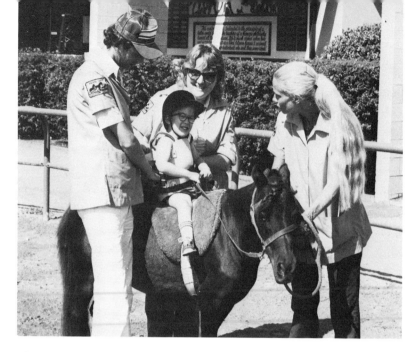

Therapeutic horseback riding at The Animal Care and Education Center in Rancho Santa Fe, California

homes; and a hot line for people whose pets die or get lost.

The Center also provides healthy animals for adoption, emergency treatment for wildlife, a twenty-four-hour lost pet locator service, and animal care and training programs. It publishes a quarterly journal and offers various seminars and workshops for teachers and other special-interest groups as well.

In addition to these activities, the Center offers an eight-week, work-study program each year for students aged fourteen to sixteen on some aspect of animal life. The 1983 program, for example, focused on horse care and stable management.

"With enough materials and programs presented in a positive light," said Golakoff, "people can then develop their own attitudes. I feel that values develop through constant reinforcement rather than by scolding people for their behavior. When we're told what not to do," Golakoff continued, smiling as he put his thoughts together, "we usually react even more negatively."

The Center's positive approach produced some exciting results recently during a special nine-week pilot program made available through a grant from the county schools.

"After the students really studied the problem of pet overpopulation in depth, and learned about the huge surplus of animals in our community alone, and how serious and wasteful it is," said Mr. Golakoff, "seven of them went home and convinced their parents that they should spay and neuter their pets.

"To me this is a perfect example of what can happen through education. When you present all the facts and show all sides of the picture, it's pretty hard to come up with any other solution."

SPREADING THE WORD

It may take some time before more shelters such as these are built. However, a number of other cities have taken a positive first step in dealing with the problem of pet overpopulation. Low-cost spay/neuter programs are beginning to spring up all over the country. Because the expense is minimal, more pet owners are taking advantage of the service.

Robert Rush, general manager of the City of Los Angeles Department of Animal Regulation, claims that although "the public low-cost spay/neuter program is not the complete answer to the problem, it does represent a vital step toward a responsible and humane approach to population control."

Unless people know about the programs and use them, however, the problem of unwanted pets will continue. Many people simply don't see the problem, don't care, or just don't realize that alternatives are available. Others don't see the connection between new puppies and kittens at their house and the staggering number of unwanted animals nationwide.

Educating people to look at new information and old beliefs in a new way, however, takes time and commitment and a willingness for each one of us to do our part.

Individual owners can help end the tragedy of unwanted pets in other ways too. By:

—observing leash and licensing laws

—becoming aware of the public health and social responsibilities of owning a pet

—finding out about the services available and using them

—encouraging friends and neighbors to do the same

POUND (PET) SEIZURE

Pound Seizure—the selling of animals from shelters to research institutions—is another way in which we abuse domestic animals.

According to the Humane Society of the United States (HSUS), the term "pound seizure" is often misused and misunderstood. Actual pound seizure laws require pounds or shelters that receive support from state or local funds to turn unclaimed dogs and cats over to researchers on demand. Only a couple of states actually have this law on their books. Others expressly forbid any release of shelter animals for research. But most states have no law on the subject. In such cases, shelters or county governments make their own rules on how unclaimed or unwanted pets will be disposed of.

Defenders of animals rights are against pound seizure because everyone suffers as a result.

1. Animal control suffers.—Due to pound seizure, shelters that normally provide a haven for lost or unwanted pets turn into "stores" where pets are sold for experiments in research labs. As a result, unwanted pets rarely find new homes, and worried owners find it almost impossible to be reunited with their lost pets before they become research tools.

2. Research results suffer.—"When a dog that's used to reg-

ular exercise, individual food preferences, and a person's companionship is thrust into a laboratory surrounding, it suffers from severe stress," said Phyllis Wright, HSUS director of Animal Sheltering and Control, in a recent issue of the Society's newletter. "The stress makes them more prone to disease and poor models for research."

Even the scientists themselves tend to agree that shelter animals, sometimes called "random-source" animals, do not make good research subjects.

Of course, there are those who claim that research would stop without the use of shelter animals. However, successful research continues in other parts of the world where using animals for research is banned. Sweden is one example. The use of random-source animals was outlawed there in 1979.

In Great Britain the use of live animals for practice surgery by medical students has been outlawed for 106 years. And again, there seems to be no indication that British surgeons are less capable than those in our country or any other.

The Fund for Animals, aggressive campaigners for outlawing pound seizure, brings the entire issue down to one question that each of us must answer for ourselves. "If my pet was lost and I couldn't find it, would I want MY PET to be sold for research?"

WHY ARE WE CRUEL TO ANIMALS?

There are many reasons why people are cruel. Cruel to one another, cruel to their environment, cruel to animals. But perhaps the main reason for cruelty to animals is the way in which people view them. Many do not regard them as creatures with feelings. Some think of pets and other animals as possessions to treat as they wish, giving little or no thought to how their treatment affects the animal itself.

Others are simply cruel. For example, one pet owner kept his dog tied up for days in the hot sun without enough fresh water and without companionship. The dog eventually died from a variety of complications—perhaps the main one being neglect.

Other pet owners have been known to lock dogs in airtight cars, chain them to trees, confine them to such small quarters that they can barely stretch or stand up, or leave them alone while they go on vacation.

Stories like these make one wonder why a person who cared so little for the animal's comfort would want a pet in the first place. Yet most pet owners are not basically cruel people. They simply don't think—or don't know.

All of these illustrations seem to return us to the same theme—education—the importance of exposing people to what is involved in taking on a pet, whether a goldfish or a golden retriever.

In many cases, people simply need a few facts and they will change their behavior. For example, a dog's cooling system is different from ours. They do not perspire. They throw off excess heat, not moisture, through the pores of their bodies. Therefore, they need plenty of circulating air on a hot day. Obviously, to confine a dog to an airtight car is an invitation to heat exhaustion—even death. Although pet handbooks are filled with such simple information, many people don't take the time to read and apply it.

I know that for a time this was true for me. As I look back, I'm shocked that I didn't know any better—but at the time I simply didn't. I allowed my Boston terrier to give birth to a litter of puppies. And though I found responsible homes for the new pups, the point is I added four more animals to the already overcrowded pet population.

And when our family cat tore some of our living room furniture to shreds, I had her front claws removed. At the time I thought it was a fair decision—certainly better than giving her away or living with tattered furniture. But it wasn't until months later when she didn't return home one morning, that I realized what a cruel thing I had done. I had robbed her of her defenses.

In both instances I thought I was acting in good faith. No one had told me anything different. And I didn't ask. So it is only now—years later and with much regret—that I see the importance of each one of us sharing what we know with those who don't yet know.

IN DEFENSE OF ANIMALS

Fortunately, there are many caring individuals, as well as dedicated organizations, who have committed themselves to defending the rights of animals and then educating others by their example.

Some are as private and unassuming as Audrey Olivera of Chula Vista, California, who has been quietly caring for unwanted cats in her home for nearly forty years.

Others are famous for their work with animals. Barbara Woodhouse, for example, is an internationally known dog trainer from Great Britain. She has spread her gospel of kindness to thousands of dogs and their owners.

And San Diego school counselor Gwen Hutchinson, and her husband, George, who share their home with fifteen cats and four dogs, grew up in a home where there was an "immense reverence for animals." Gwen claims she has been a defender of animals since she was ten years old. And she now runs her own personal adoption service.

Although these three women may never meet, they share with each other a love and compassion for animals that has affected everyone they've come in contact with.

CAT LADY RETIRES

Today at the age seventy-nine, Audrey Olivera, affectionately known as the "Cat Lady," plans to retire after nearly a lifetime of service to stray cats.

During the 1950s Mrs. Olivera and her husband provided a

Audrey Olivera of Chula Vista, California, and part of her "cat family"

home for as many as two hundred cats at a time—those that had been "dumped," abandoned on the mesa.

"I don't know how people can just dump cats and kittens, or any animal," said Mrs. Olivera. "Some people just don't have hearts. They do the same thing with dogs. I'm just trying to help the good Lord."

Visitors claim her home is clean and odorless. She keeps twenty litter boxes in the laundry room and cleans them twice a day. And she has had all of the cats neutered by Mercy Crusade or Pet Assistance, two San Diego groups that provide low-cost neutering.

After a recent illness, she told a reporter that she just can't continue caring for such a large brood. Over a period of time she will gradually cut down her cat family from fifty-two to seventeen. "I'll keep just the old ones," she says.

Friends of Cats, a nonprofit organization in San Diego that finds homes for cats has agreed to take thirty of the animals.

THE GOSPEL OF KINDNESS

On the other side of the world, famous dog trainer Barbara Woodhouse, "in her familiar pleated skirt and sensible brown loafers" as one reporter noted, might be mistaken for the local librarian or head schoolmistress. But instead the charming sixtyish woman has spent the past twenty years training more than seventeen thousand dogs. In fact, she has been so successful that the *Guinness Book of World Records* lists her as the most successful trainer in the world.

"I love spreading the gospel of kindness and quickness," she says of herself and her work. "Jerk 'em and love 'em, that's my motto."

The message of her British television series and her new book, *No Bad Dogs the Woodhouse Way*, (New York: Summit Books) proclaims that anyone who is willing to learn how to approach dogs properly, maintain eye contact with them, and encourage

Noted British dog trainer, Barbara Woodhouse, gives some obedience tips to an audience in Chicago, Illinois.

them with a variety of voices can be as successful as she is.

"A pat and a kind word are not enough in the initial training of dogs," she reveals in her book. "The atmosphere must be charged with a certain excitement . . . dogs love laughter, clapping and jokes . . . You can't train a dog well if you are unhappy."

During her childhood, Barbara Woodhouse claims she had a kind of "telepathy" or thought transference with animals. She spent much of her growing up years talking to dogs and taking them for walks. She was also, in her words, "mad for horses," and in college rode with the Oxford University Polo Club.

LOVER OF LIFE

Gwen Hutchinson is another gentle woman who has a special affinity for animals. Gwen not only loves animals—actually, all creatures—she also loves to talk about them and, more important, to do something for them. "What I personally have learned from working with and living with animals, even the tiniest little bird, is my humanness, my warmth. All I want to do is teach people gentleness and the education of the heart.

"This is not something I learned from the outer world," added the warm and friendly woman, a school counselor by profession, "it's something I learned directly from animals."

Of herself, she said, smiling, "I think I was born being a lover of life. When I was about ten years of age, I decided I'd be a defender of animals. I just grew into it. My dogs and cats became my children. I never liked dolls."

Then at age fourteen, Gwen learned a great deal about the care and responsibility of pets from her new stepmother. She taught Gwen the practical and medical side of owning a pet. "I learned from her that when you take on an animal you look to see what there is to do. It's more than just feeding and playing with them."

Gwen left home at nineteen, married and moved to Los Angeles with her husband. "On payday," she said, recalling her early married years with a smile, "I'd buy a six-pack of cat food for a dollar and feed all the alley cats." At first, Gwen felt she was doing a really worthwhile thing for the hungry little critters. But she soon learned something she's never forgotten.

"I learned," she cautioned, using her hands for emphasis, "that I wasn't being truly responsible. I saw that most of the cats were full of disease because they were living in an environment that didn't support life. Therefore, the food I gave them wasn't enough. They needed medical care as well."

So Gwen decided to get involved with an organization called Volunteer Services to Animals, an activist group that was ded-

Gwen Hutchinson of San Diego

icated to breaking down the communication problems that were going on within the area of animal regulation. "I was trained to move volunteers into the pounds and shelters to help reunite lost pets and worried owners."

Then in the early 70s, the Hutchinsons moved to San Diego where Gwen has continued her work with animals as a private citizen. Although she has been involved with shelters and pounds to some extent, she admits that she prefers to do what needs to be done in her own way.

Gwen was quick to admit that in deciding to use her home as a base for her work, it didn't mean she found fault with particular individuals. She realizes the system, for the most part, just doesn't work. "For example," she said, in talking about the people who work at the shelters, "if you're overworked, you almost forget what you're there for. I just couldn't continue to watch what goes on in most shelters." People's attitudes seemed to reflect the crowded conditions, lack of funds, limited employees, and so on.

"It's as though people seem to be saying, 'I'd better hurry up before somebody crawls on my case.' 'Go through and hose down. It doesn't really matter who gets wet.' 'Act like you don't see that there's a mother animal delivering her babies on a cold floor.' 'Pretend you don't know that the euthanasia chamber doesn't work effectively—half-alive bodies thrown on the dump.'

"I admit that I too pretended not to see everything that went on. Let's face it, a shelter will never be a home. And over a period of time, when workers find their jobs painful and they don't feel supported and their budget is always in the red, well, pretty soon they become indifferent to what's going on."

As a result, Gwen decided to change her approach. She began keeping strays in her home and then putting them up for adoption by networking through veterinarians. She also talks to people about adopting animals wherever she goes.

"I schedule a three- to four-hour screening process with every prospective owner," said Gwen. "I teach them about disease, care, feeding. I give them books to read on how to keep their animal healthy. And I talk with them about the major things a pet needs on a regular basis, such as proper diet and veterinary care. I also let them know which organizations to call for financial assistance if they get into an emergency.

"I know that what I do has integrity," Gwen added, leaning forward in her chair, brown curls framing her friendly face. "The rewards come from the wonderful success stories I hear from the people who adopt my animals. I have the satisfaction of knowing that for every animal I bring in and process out again, it now has a loving home. That's—well, it's WOW!

"I also feel that adults have a responsibility to teach children about animal overpopulation—what really happens to cats and dogs who have litters. Kids should know that when they pass out free kittens or give away little puppies (in front of a market

Children viewing animals up for adoption at the San Diego County Humane Society

or along the beach) out of total ignorance, they just add to the millions of pets that are killed every year because someone didn't care what happened to them.

"I also feel that if children were given that information—if they really knew the percentage of pets that are destroyed because of indifference and ignorance—they would pass on what they learned. They would quickly see that those who are educated need to teach those who are afraid just as someone taught them. Children really are the keepers of the peace," she added softly.

Then pointing to some printed materials in front of her, she continued, "Just look at pound seizure. It's nothing but a political ball game in the hands of money. But if you took a group of thirteen and fourteen year olds through the laboratories I've seen, pound seizure would end today because these young people wouldn't let it rest.

"Kids give no importance to titles or figures or money. They don't care about political pressure either. If they saw what I've seen and really understood that no animal leaves a research lab— ever—I know what they'd say. 'If that's what they do in labs, there's got to be a better way. Don't hurt the animals.' And then they'd set out to find a better way."

Chapter Three
The Price of Pleasure

Zoos, circuses, rodoes, horse racing, movies, and television. Americans take their pick of this great variety of entertainment each week. All are familiar forms of fun to adults and children alike. But for most of the animals involved, it's anything but fun. Many die needless deaths or at best, live their lives in confinement and discomfort just so human beings can satisfy their need to be entertained.

THE HOLLYWOOD WAY

For example, during the filming of *The Capture of Grizzly Adams* for NBC in 1981, producers used brutal wires known as running W's to force horses to the ground for specific action scenes.

While shooting *Heaven's Gate*, filmmakers staged a vicious cockfight for a full week, though they needed only about three or four minutes of suitable footage.

"The Chisholms," filmed for CBS near Springfield, Illinois, resulted in the killing of four animals for no reason. One of the lines of dialogue required someone to hold up two rabbits and

Simulation, using ropes, of "running W's," which are used to trip horses in films.

two ducks and say, "Look, I just shot our supper."

A couple of bundles of fur could have worked just as well— with no loss of reality. The viewers would not have known the difference. But instead they used live animals—each one killed by a karate chop to its neck just before shooting the scene.

"No matter how much realism you're striving to achieve," said Carmelita Pope, director of the American Humane Association's Hollywood chapter, in a recent newspaper account, "there's just never any excuse for actually abusing an animal on the set. It's so needless. Our credo is that you should never harm an animal for the sake of a motion picture or a television program."

The group has been working to protect animals in the movie industry since 1939 when a horse was killed during the shooting of the film *Jesse James*.

"They made this horse run on a greased plank to the edge of

a cliff," said Ms. Pope. "Then they pulled the plank out from under him, and the horse fell forty feet to his death in a small body of water."

Following that incident the AHA sent one of its agents to Hollywood to protest what was happening, and to begin protecting animals used in films. That marked the start of the work the organization continues to do on behalf of animal actors.

Today, the AHA is backed by the New Screen Actors Guild contract which gives them power to enforce their animal-safety rules. However, because there are no penalties for violations, some producers ignore the contract and go on abusing their animals.

One bear handler, for example, boasted that he could get his bear to do anything on camera. How? By withholding food for a month before filming started. Other handlers poke, prod, or taunt their animals in order to get the response they want— particularly for ferocious fights or battle sequences.

AHA does recognize that some animal cruelty scenes may be necessary to the story line, but they insist that these can be filmed in such a way that the real animal actors are not hurt. In other words, the final shooting may include sequences that appear violent to the audience, but in fact, do not require mistreating the animals off-camera.

For example, *Blazing Saddles*, *The Black Marble*, and *Cat People* are a few movies that do contain some cruel scenes— without the use of actual cruelty. In fact, the animals were treated humanely on set and each of the movies received full cooperation from the AHA.

DAREDEVIL/REALITY PROGRAMS

More recently, a variety of daredevil and so-called reality programs are being filmed for television. "Those Amazing Animals," for example, showed many predatory scenes—animals killing other animals. Although this is a natural part of wildlife

41

behavior, explained Ms. Pope, "Sometimes I got the impression that animals were deliberately put in that position so the producers would have some exciting action footage. Of course, it's difficult to prove something like that."

The AHA has also received many angry complaints about the series "You Asked For It." Viewers are outraged at some of the gruesome segments. According to one report, in one show they actually "threw a lamb into a tank of piranha, and then filmed the animal being torn apart."

Ms. Pope added that the organization has judged only forty-some films as unacceptable over the past few years—"not a terribly large amount," she said. "The movie and TV industry generally do all of their 'animal action' in a very humane manner. But there are still some persons who seem to have no respect for animals."

The producer of *The Legend of the Lone Ranger*, for example, refused to let the staff of AHA on their set in New Mexico and Utah. When Ms. Pope asked him how they planned to shoot a scene which involved a savage fight between a buffalo and a horse, "He said it was none of my business. It was a very frustrating situation."

MIXED FEELINGS ABOUT ZOOS

Zoos are another area of entertainment that draws mixed reviews. "The last time I was at a zoo," said Gwen Hutchinson, "I watched a man poking the tigers with a stick just so he could get the action shot he wanted. At that moment I wondered who was really in the cage. My work with animals keeps me looking at humans and our condition."

John Sparks, zoologist and TV producer of the fascinating 1982 PBS nature series "The Discovery of Animal Behavior," seems to hold a similar view.

"I have mixed feelings about zoos," he told one reporter. "I think for someone sitting in New York to be able to have a place

Sitatunga antelope in Cascade Canyon, one of the natural habitats at the San Diego Zoo

where he can actually see an elephant and smell it is wonderful. But wildlife parks are better than traditional zoos, even though some zoos claim to be preserving species."

Sparks feels that it's very rare for any zoo to save a species from extinction. "Few animals ever breed in captivity beyond two or three generations," he added.

In his opinion, the only way to save the endangered is to preserve their habitat. "Man has to intervene in some way so that certain areas are kept sacrosanct for the animals. That's the only reasonable way." In the long run, Sparks feels it is up to each one of us to be responsible for our growing economies. At some point we'll have to bring the human population in line so that we can better share the earth.

As for Mr. Sparks' contribution to animal/human relations, he dedicated himself to producing a television series that would bring the world of animals to people in a very positive way.

His "Nature" miniseries concentrated on the little-known aspects of wildlife behavior—bird migration, humanlike pet tricks, and the honeybee's successful search for nectar, as well as some fascinating insights into how animals "think" and develop imagination.

Meanwhile, the controversy over zoos continues. As people become more aware of animal rights and welfare, the more questions they ask.

Dale Jamieson, a philosopher from the University of Colorado, for example, raises many important points in a paper he recently wrote on captive animals. "Most zoos ought to be abolished, not just because they demean animals, but also because they demean humans," he said.

Then with a bit of twisted humor, he added, "Most children first encounter an animal between two slices of bread."

Jamieson feels that zoos have led to greater separation between animals and humans. He sees it as a kind of slavery which hurts both people and animals.

Gwen Hutchinson tends to agree. "Living with animals is natural," she claims. And it's obvious that she means what she says, as her own cats crawl contentedly between her feet, then stretch peacefully in front of the sunny window of her very lived-in living room.

"I truly feel there's an underlying human need to be with animals," she added, "but we've put it together that it isn't."

Zoos, for example, in Gwen's view, support this myth. In the past zoos have been so preoccupied with exotics and endangered species that they practically ignore local wildlife.

"Many zoos are just now beginning to look at extending their scope. For too long they have continued to work out of solutions they already had. My whole concern," she continued, leaning back in her chair for a moment of thought, "is to break out of that box of old beliefs and begin looking at solving our problem from a bigger perspective."

We can't really progress until we give up doing things the same old way. It hasn't worked so far so why do we keep repeating our mistakes? This is the question more and more people are beginning to ask.

"When I really got how precious life is," said Gwen, "I got it across the board." All forms of life deserve our reverence, not just a few privileged groups.

IS THE PRICE TOO GREAT?

Ivan Golakoff, who worked in a zoo for many years before joining The Animal Care and Education Center, feels that zoos are not always as sensitive to the needs of the animals as the public might believe. "A great deal of money is spent on painting, showing, and other things," he said, "but the animals themselves are not always housed properly."

Golakoff sees nothing wrong with small groups of animals dedicated to educating people about their native species. "I suppose the sacrifice of a few captive animals used to teach people how to develop their sense of responsibility for them is worth the sacrifice. But unless the zoo is run properly with the needs of the animals kept in focus, no one benefits."

Golakoff talked for a moment about wild animal parks. Although they provide a good home for animals while in captivity, he feels that most of the species are overprotected. As a result, "Genes are weakened because the animals are not allowed to live out their natural instincts."

In other words, in the wild the "marginal" or weaker of the species would be killed by predators in the natural order of things. "But when man interferes and starts playing games with nature," added Golakoff, "the natural order is disturbed."

In a peculiar kind of way our zeal for saving endangered species may actually work against them in the long run. Will we save some only to mutate (change the genes which will affect heredity) them at the same time?

ANOTHER SIDE OF THE STORY

Robert O. Wagner, executive director of the American Association of Zoological Parks and Aquariums (AAZPA), says that in many ways he would tend to agree with some of the criticism leveled at zoos, "except for the new awareness which has swept 'zoodom' in the last five to ten years."

In 1982 alone, zoos and aquariums in the United States and Canada spent $130 million for more natural habitat. Among them the San Diego Zoo, known for its many beautiful and innovative displays, recently completed its new multimillion dollar primate exhibit.

Today more and more zoos are also collecting animals in breeding colonies instead of displaying just one or two of a kind in a sterile cage.

Mr. Wagner says that zoos can help humans to develop a reverence for animals. In fact, the animals themselves, he feels, become "ambassadors for their kind still in the wild."

The world's best zoos educate people about various animals, support scientific research, and help preserve endangered species.

Viewing captive animals might be educational, claims philosopher Jamieson, "But what does it teach us?" he asks. "It teaches us a false sense of our place in the natural order."

He believes it produces people who think they can live successfully in a human community and human world, and simply use animals to satisfy their own selfish needs, if indeed they bother with them at all.

NOTHING SHORT OF EXCELLENCE

Warren Thomas, doctor of veterinary medicine and director of the world-famous Los Angeles Zoo, sees things another way. He turned a once motley collection of sterile cages and caves into one of the finest zoos in the world. The exhibits and habitats in Los Angeles are some of the most attractive and imaginative anywhere.

A beautiful waterfall graces the gorilla section, while the wild goats can climb a craggy castle.

"Everything this zoo does must be synonymous with excellence," says Thomas. "These people," he adds, referring to his dedicated staff, "are ready to put out the extra mile. They are a highly motivated, carefully screened group of the crème de la crème and that's why our force is so good."

Thomas then returns to his main focus, the animals themselves. "We feel strongly that in order to do justice to the animals within our care, we must use the full spectrum of scientific procedures available. We are morally bound to care for and foster these animals. It is a trust."

FUN OR PROFIT?

From the quiet outdoor zoo to the noisy indoor setting of a modern-day rodeo is quite a trip. Picture the scene. A large arena full of excited, shouting fans. The smell of horses and sawdust. The aroma of hot dogs. The salty taste of buttered popcorn. Bright lights and music. Riders decked out in colorful shirts and ties, and broad-brimmed western hats.

Horses, calves, and bulls pushing against the chutes. Real cowboys roping steers. Cowgirls chasing barrels. Calves brought to the ground without a second wasted. Just like the old days. A touch of Americana! Let the show begin.

In truth, however, "The modern American rodeo bears little resemblance to early competitions where working cowboys tested their range skills after roundups," according to The Humane Society of the United States. Professional rodeos today take place in modern arenas "where horses, calves, and bulls are roped, pushed, kicked, shocked, and otherwise abused" to entertain the crowd.

Behind the bright lights and music, the plain truth is, rodeos are high-powered and dangerous—for rider as well as animal. And they're big business too. The risks are high but so are the earnings. The men and women involved, however, have a choice. The animals do not.

Most lead lives linked to constant pain and injury. Between events, and on the road between cities, rodeo animals spend most of their time nose-to-tail in crowded corrals, trucks, and trailers.

Take a look at what goes on in the name of entertainment.

BRONC-RIDING

One of the few rodeo events that can be traced to the past is a cowboy's ability to stay on the back of a bucking horse. To be able to break a wild horse quickly and turn it into a ridable mount was important in times when horses were the main means of transportation.

But today, the original purpose has been twisted into a cruel fate for unfortunate rodeo horses. Riders must wear and use spurs

Bareback bronc riding at the Lakeside Rodeo in San Diego County

throughout the ride. In fact, the more a horse bucks the higher the score. To make sure the horse bucks, riders fasten a leather cinch, called a flank strap, to the horse's sensitive abdomen. Although cowboys claim that the horse bucks because it wants to get rid of the rider, the truth is that the horse bucks because it is in pain. And it stops not because the rider is thrown off or jumps off, but because the painful strap is finally released.

CALF ROPING

In this event, a cowboy tests his ability to rope a calf and tie it up as fast as he can. Sure, the calf is given a head start— forced ahead, actually—after its tail has been twisted or its back zapped with an electric prod.

The cowboy then gallops full speed and stops within roping distance. As the calf hits its top speed, the cowboy tightens the rope around its neck and snaps the animal to the ground. Next he grabs the calf and ties its legs together.

Though the event may last only fifteen seconds, it's frightening for the animal. And unlike a similar event in early western days, there is no thought about whether or not the calf is injured or even killed in the process.

BULL RIDING

This event is considered the most dangerous, yet the most exciting too—for obvious reasons. Shoved into a tiny fenced-in chute, the bull stands, roped around its girth and across its genitals.

While waiting to be released, someone continually shocks him with an electric cattle prod. Then when the chute is finally opened the animal charges violently into the arena. No wonder. At last, escape from torment. High in the grandstand, however, spectators are led to believe that the bull is angry at the cowboy. And as skilled announcers draw the audience's attention to what comes next, no one is the wiser about how the event was put together in the first place.

STEER WRESTLING

Man against animal in hand-to-horn combat. Called bulldogging or steer wrestling, this cruel event began when its inventor realized that a bulldog could subdue a steer by biting its upper lip. Today's event, however, is quite a departure from the original version.

Mounted cowboys in modern arenas chase the steer out of the chute, fall on top of the animal, and then twist its neck viciously until it is thrown to the ground. The faster the cowboy completes the process, the higher the score. And once again, no one is concerned with the welfare of the animal. Speed and accuracy are all that matters.

OTHER EVENTS

Steer busting involves an animal being jerked off its feet with a rope. And team steer-roping is a cruel kind of tug-of-war event where one rider lassos the animal's head or horns and another its hind feet. Each cowboy then pulls in the opposite direction.

Although rodeo professionals claim these animals are being saved from the slaughterhouse, it appears to be only a temporary saving. After they have outlived their lives as performers, most of them end up on someone's plate after all.

WHAT ARE THE ALTERNATIVES?

Is it reasonable to think rodeos will ever be anything but what they are now? Or that zoos will only open in major areas or regions where there is enough money and interest to support the kind of life and habitats the animals deserve? Or that the movie and television industry will finally realize that brutality and entertainment do not necessarily go together?

And what about cock and bull fighting? And circuses? And magic shows? And horse and dog racing? Does our pleasure really depend upon degrading our fellow creatures?

Do you think it's possible for us to simply enjoy animals just as they are—for what they are? Or must we continue to change them and use them and exploit them? Would we be willing to learn from them? To observe them and to study them without intruding on their way of life?

What are our alternatives? Or perhaps a better question is, what are the animals' alternatives? Perhaps if we ever really communicated with them—at the level of heart—we might come up with some surprising answers.

What might those be? How about an educational fair in which the animals are the stars instead of the slaves of the show? Where people could learn about the past, the customs, the folklore and the important part horses and cattle played in early America.

51

Where education and entertainment were one. Where children and adults could see and touch and experience their heritage through displays and exhibits. Where we could learn by observing the magnificence of the animals, instead of sitting in bleachers or in front of a screen gawking at clever performers tricking and trapping them into action for the sake of a few cheap thrills and a few dollars.

It seems that our entire view of animals and entertainment needs a whole new perspective—a world vision, based on love and respect for all of life, instead of just our narrow little view. We need to stop using animals for our own selfish ends. Exploiting them just because they can't speak up for themselves. Amusing ourselves at their expense because we're too lazy or blind or indifferent to their right to lives that are in keeping with their natures.

Only when each one of us sees our individual responsibility for the problems will this brutality and waste come to an end. Meanwhile, perhaps it is the job of those who know and care to monitor those who don't care until we all learn to be more humane.

Chapter Four
Farm or Factory?

When I was a child, one of my favorite Sunday outings was a drive to my uncle's small chicken farm in Orland Park, Illinois. Hens and chicks scrambled at our feet as we ran through the yard. Tall golden corn grew above our heads in the nearby fields. And if we behaved and helped set the table and clean up afterwards, there was always Aunt Madeline's homemade apple or cherry pie and ice cream for dessert.

In the years since, my aunt and uncle have sold their farm, moved to the city, and eventually retired to Southern California. But my memories of those cozy family gatherings will be with me forever.

For many Americans, *memories* of traditional farmlife are all they have. A trip to a farm for today's young person would be closer to a tour of a factory, where animals, like so many coats, or pairs of shoes, or pieces of furniture are checked in, labeled, processed, and shipped.

There are still some small farms and ranches raising their animals in the traditional way. On most farms, however, chickens no longer run free, but instead live out their short lives in battery cages so small their feet often grow around the wire floors because they are unable to move.

Young calves, like those that once nuzzled their mothers in sunny pastures, are now weaned soon after birth and isolated in small darkened pens without room enough to stretch or turn around.

Computers, vacuum pumps, automated feeders, and specially designed, wire-mesh floors have replaced the family farmer, the quiet streams, open meadows, sunny pastures, and the familiar henyard of the past. Though some traditional farms still remain, most owners are quick to admit that it's downright tough to stay in existence against the competition of the giant "agribusiness" known as factory farming.

WHAT IS FACTORY FARMING?

A factory farm is a large, automated operation which practices "intensive livestock husbandry," as they say in the business. Animals, treated as machines, are raised in overcrowded, artificial environments for only one purpose—to produce goods that will earn a profit.

On factory farms, the animal's nature, needs, and right to life are not considered. All that matters is the end result—a profit from high volume sales of meat, eggs, and dairy products.

When we select our hamburger, steaks, frying chickens, or pork chops from the supermarket showcase, most of us give little or no thought to the suffering of the live animals involved.

Most of us just haven't known any better. We haven't thought about it, or discussed it, or had any information to help us make an informed choice. Most of us have grown up eating meat and dairy products every day—bacon and eggs for breakfast, hamburgers and hot dogs for lunch, steak or fried chicken for dinner.

Yet, we are probably the same people who are outraged if a

pet dog is locked in a closed car, a bird is poked out of its nest, or a sick cat is abandoned by the side of the road.

Desmond Morris, a well-known ethologist and author of many books on human and animal behavior, recently wrote a beautiful editorial for *Fact Sheet*, newsletter of the Food Animal Concerns Trust. He talked about this very thing—the inconsistency of our behavior toward pets and wildlife, and animals raised for food.

> Somewhere along the line those long-suffering servants of ours, the food-producing farm animals, have lost out. Their lot has actually worsened, while the others (domestics and wildlife) have been treated with more care and respect. . . .
> Most of us live with this inconsistency because, although we see the wild creatures and the pets, we do not see the unfortunate battery creatures—whether hens, pigs, or calves—because they are neatly shut away from view in anonymous private buildings . . . The moral of this story, if you happen to be a bird or a mammal, is not to provide mankind with any valuable form of food. If you merely provide companionship as a pet, or beauty as a wild creature, you will be well treated; but if you give more—if you provide your eggs, or your meat, for human sustenance— your reward will be a life sentence in an animal concentration camp.

LAYERS AND BROILERS

Chickens are some of the many animals that live in the concentration camps Morris speaks of. In fact, today, over 90 percent of all chickens are raised on factory farms for two basic purposes—to lay eggs or to be broiled as meat. "Layers" or egg-hens, under normal conditions, could live from fifteen to twenty years. Raised the factory-farming way, however, they last only about a year and a half.

During their short lives they are confined in cages stacked three or four stories high in large commercial buildings. These

An egg factory

wire-mesh cages, without perches, are usually eighteen to twenty inches square and hold three to four birds each.

The cage floor slants to allow the eggs to roll through an opening onto a conveyor belt that moves them to a special processing room. There workers wash, grade, pack, and store the eggs. Conveyor belts also bring food and water to the chickens.

Bird droppings from upper cages fall on sheet-metal boards mounted over the lower cages. A power-driven assembly moves the waste to a pit below. And when the material accumulates in the pit, another scraper pushes it out of the building.

The birds exist under such stressful conditions that after several months they begin to produce fewer eggs. As a result, they are no longer worth the cost to feed and keep them. When their time is up, they are used for soup or pet food.

Broiler chickens are also raised in confinement. Shortly after birth, workers clip the beaks and toes of young chicks to prevent pecking and fighting. At first, they are housed at one end of the building under bright lights to encourage feeding. Then after a couple of weeks, they are moved onto the entire floor. Heaters, automatic feeders and waterers run the length of the building.

It takes about eight weeks before the birds are ready for market. During the last few weeks, when the floor is the most crowded, many farms dim the lights to reduce fighting. When the flock is ready to be slaughtered, birds are forced to one end of the building. At night, when the chickens are less flighty, crews of "catchers" enter the building, catch them, and load them into crates on waiting trucks.

Catching the birds by hand is considered expensive, since it takes time and human labor. However, at this point, broilers cannot be raised in cages. Caged birds develop bruises and blisters easily, and often have leg and foot problems as well. These injuries spoil their meat. But the broiler industry is not easily discouraged. They are now trying to find a more effective way to raise and capture the birds.

One equipment firm in England may have found the answer—cages with a drop-away floor that would dump the broilers onto a conveyor belt.

Life in the crowded sheds seems unbearable enough. But the real travesty begins after the birds are caught and caged and

Hens in battery cages

moved to the processing plants. At that point, the "hanging crew" lifts the birds from the crates and hangs them by both feet on a conveyor.

They travel this way for several minutes. At first, the birds flap their wings frantically. But as the blood rushes to their heads, they quiet down. Next they pass over a stunner and receive an electric shock through the head and neck.

Unless the birds are stunned, some continue to flap their wings at slaughter time and cause their meat to be damaged. After a few more feet of travel, they pass through an automatic slaughter device. This channel positions the necks as they move through a radial saw. Because some birds lift their heads out of the channel, an operator stands by and cuts their necks with a sharp knife. The conveyor then passes over an area where the birds bleed out completely before being moved into hot water scalders.

More than 3 billion chickens in the United States alone live and die this way each year. Ducks and turkeys are no better off. Most are mass-produced the same way.

RABBITS ARE NEXT

Southern-fried rabbit, Bucket O' Bunny—whatever you want to call it, using rabbits for food is the latest trend. Rabbit factory farms are on the rise. And according to a report in *People Weekly*, April 3, 1983, the Hopper may soon replace the Whopper.

Richard Stewart, founder of Hop-Scotch in West Lafayette, Indiana, claims that his is the nation's first fried rabbit restaurant. At first, he received a slew of hate letters and calls, but as far as he's concerned, eating rabbit is no worse than eating veal or lamb. "Anybody who's ever seen a baby calf or a lamb," says Stewart, "knows that they're cute little things, too."

He opened his small diner just two blocks from Purdue University in January, 1983, and has already had to expand his eating area. To meet the growing demand, Stewart fries a hundred rabbits a day.

He also expects to earn about $300,000 this year—ten times his original investment. And if success continues, Stewart plans to set up franchises in other cities, as well.

PORK—ANOTHER WORD FOR PIG

A good roll in the mud is almost a thing of the past for today's pig. In fact, most of them are lucky to ever see the light of day. About 90 percent of all U.S. pork is processed through some kind of confinement system.

Pregnant sows live in large sheds, confined to cramped stalls with concrete floors and slats for waste material. As with chickens, pig farmers keep the barns dark to reduce stress. Just before giving birth, the sow is moved to a farrowing stall until the piglets are born. The stall is just large enough for her to stand or lie down. She cannot walk or turn around. In addition, the farmer chains the sow in place so she will not accidentally lie down on one of her sucklings and crush it.

On some farms the piglets are born in confinement, then

Sow with piglets in farrowing crate

Young pig chewing aimlessly on the wire of its cage.

moved to outdoor pens or pasture. The trend, however, is toward larger mass-production methods similar to those used with chickens. Farms already using this method raise their pigs in total confinement—from birth to slaughterhouse. And agricultural experts predict that by 1985, up to 70 percent of all pigs will be raised this way.

And no wonder, when farmers and employees are encouraged to take the following attitude: "The breeding sow should be thought of, and treated as, a valuable piece of machinery whose function is to pump out baby pigs like a sausage machine." (L.J. Taylor, export development manager for The Wall's Meat Company, Ltd., in *National Hog Farmer*, March, 1978.)

Results may yield higher pork profits for the farmer. But what about the pig? In addition to its life, it must also give up free movement, fresh air, and contact with peers during the short life permitted.

"GOURMET VEAL"

Young calves, however, are perhaps the most mistreated of all factory-farm animals. Their tender, white meat commands a high price in the market and in restaurants. And breeders and farmers know it. So they do whatever is necessary to satisfy the "gourmet" taste. But the cost to the young calf has caused one of the biggest controversies the meat industry has known.

The system used to raise prime veal may well be the harshest form of confinement. And as consumers demand more and more veal, the industry continues to grow.

For example, in 1981–82, Burger King, known for its mammoth hamburgers, added a new specialty to their menu—the veal parmigiana sandwich. A coalition of seventy animal rights groups went up in arms over this abuse. Representatives picketed Burger King in twenty major United States cities, including New York, Washington, Chicago, and Miami. They claimed that veal is "the most cruelly produced of all meat" and wanted the chain to stop serving this sandwich.

Since then, Burger King has withdrawn the sandwich from more than two-thirds of their outlets. And according to a recent report in *Vegetarian Times*, coalition members stated that their campaign played an important part in this decision.

Veal in many forms, however, appears on menus in thousands of restaurants around the world, so why has the coalition come down so hard on Burger King? Animal rights representatives claim that since Burger King is the second largest fast-food chain in the world, their menu could influence other chains. They fear that once people get a taste for this meat, the demand will rise.

Meanwhile, to meet even the current demand for veal, most newborn calves are taken from their mothers at an early age and totally confined in two-foot-by-four-foot stalls. Many live in darkness up to twenty-two hours a day to keep them from kicking or banging themselves against the bars which could "ruin" their meat. Food consists of a liquid diet deficient in iron in order to produce anemia. This condition results in the milky-white meat so highly prized by gourmets.

Authors Jim Mason and Peter Singer, while researching ma-

Veal calf in a crate

Boredom often results in abnormal behavior such as tongue-rolling in cattle.

terial for their recent book *Animal Factories*, visited a milk-fed veal factory in northern Connecticut.

"In two rooms, more than a hundred calves were crated in rows of wooden stalls," the men reported. "Their eyes followed our movements; some appeared jittery, others lethargic. Many tried to stretch toward us from their stalls in an attempt to suck a finger, a hand, or part of our clothing. The farmer explained, 'They want their mothers, I guess.' "

Their lives continue in this way for fifteen weeks. Producers would like to keep the calves longer so they would gain more weight. But by this time the anemia is so severe that many are already close to death. Others have already died. If kept longer, more could become ill and die.

BEEF AND MILKING COWS

According to the Animal Protection Institute of America, "About half of all dairy cows are now kept in some type of confinement system." "Free stall" barns allow the cows to move from their barns on concrete floors. In "tie stall" barns, however, cows remain in one place, chained to their stalls at the necks—sometimes for months at a time. Milking machines are brought to them.

After each calf is born, cows give milk for about ten months. To increase milk production, farmers usually rebreed by artificial insemination (placing semen in the reproductive organs of the female) as soon as possible after each birth.

"Although feedlots and confinement systems have fallen slightly in number," says API, "they are still very much a part of the U.S. beef production process."

FARMERS UNDER STRESS

Many ranchers still raise free range cattle, but for some it is beginning to require too much land and labor for too little profit. Increasing their volume is the only choice most traditional farmers have if they are to continue to pay their bills and support their families. The farmer who decides to stay small seems to be paving the way to bankruptcy.

But even if they choose factory-farming methods, the expense can still be overwhelming. Setting up a pig-confinement system, for example, can cost up to $1,500 for each breeding sow. And a family-size dairy can run about $200,000. These figures cover the cost of buildings and equipment alone. Farmland is extra.

To keep up with the trends then, farmers must devote more and more time to the financial affairs than ever before. Some go to night school to learn new methods and marketing techniques. Others have less time on the land than they used to—the reason many of them chose farming in the first place.

The farmers themselves admit that their problems and worries are more complex than ever. One Kansas farmer told a re-

Arthur and Carolyn Alford are doubtful about the future of independent ranches, as they survey their Mesa Grande cattle ranch near San Diego. Dog Moxy looks on.

porter for *New York* magazine that he'd love to have a small farm again but it seemed out of his hands. "I'm from the generation that took to farming because of the life-style, and if we made a living that was okay. The best time I ever had farming was when I used horses and came home every evening at five to help Eileen in the vegetable garden. But there's no time anymore."

Despite pressure from the mass farming movement, however, there are still some people who see real value in running a small, family-size, diversified farm. And many manage to turn a good profit without the huge investment of money and automation needed to run a factory farm. In fact, many are outraged at the lack of social and ethical responsibility shown by those who have gone the way of "agribusiness."

TRANSPORTATION AND SLAUGHTER

Another cruel aspect of factory farming involves transportation. Livestock are moved many times before they reach the slaughterhouse. Overcrowding, rough handling, stress, and extreme heat and cold cause many deaths. To the farmers, the losses amount to millions of dollars each year.

Humane slaughter laws state that an animal be stunned before slaughter to eliminate pain. But where no state laws exist or where they are not enforced, axemen wield a poleax or sledgehammer device to kill them. Kosher slaughter (to meet the requirements of Jewish law) involves hoisting fully conscious animals onto conveyor belts. Their jugular vein and windpipe are then cut with a knife.

The pain and suffering of these methods can hardly be ignored. Yet, how many of us have been aware of what really goes on in preparing our meat for the table?

As Dick Gregory says in his book *The Shadow That Scares Me*, "Animals and humans suffer and die alike. If you had to kill your own hog before you ate it, most likely you would not be able to do it . . . so you get the man down at the packing-house to do the killing for you."

"THE STAIRWAY TO HEAVEN"

Temple Grandin of Tempe, Arizona, a specialist in livestock handling, is one person who has worked to ease the plight of livestock in slaughterhouses. She helped design a humane slaughtering system called "The Stairway to Heaven," in the Swift Fresh Meat Plant in Tolleson, Arizona.

Here soothing music calms the cattle as they walk up a kind of moving sidewalk. The stairway leads to a V-shape, conveyorized, restraining chute. Then before the animal knows what's happening, the conveyor hoists it up, holding it in place along the entire sides of its body. While still in the restrainer, the animal is instantly knocked unconscious with a captive-bolt stunner. The entire process, according to those who use it, eliminates cruelty, panic, injury, and loss.

Many people, however, are against the killing of animals for food—period. To them, no method, regardless of how calm and soothing we make it, can justify that fact.

A REPORT FROM BRITAIN

The United States is not the only country where animals are raised in confinement. And citizens in our nation are not the only ones waking up to the complex problem.

Great Britain has also had its share of animal machines. But, "There is a limit to the way in which we can make animals into machines," said Sir William Elliott, chairman of the House of Commons Agriculture Committee. "They're not machines."

Elliott and his committee investigated factory-farming methods in Britain, and in 1981 shocked the British food industry with its bans on inhumane practices.

—Pigs and sows must not be raised in darkness or solitary confinement.

66

—Farms should give solid food to cattle and straw bedding to pigs.

—Pens should allow calves enough room to groom themselves, turn around, and lie comfortably.

—Battery cages, now holding 95 percent of all of England's chickens, are to be totally abolished by 1985.

The committee admitted that prices would rise because of the new plan, but said that Britons would be willing to pay an extra shilling or so to rescue the chickens from such degrading lives.

Sir William is not simply a politician making laws. He knows what he's talking about. He raises livestock himself. And he realizes that his own farm will be less efficient under the new standards. But, he concluded, "The philosophy of the human-animal relationship was very much in our minds," as the committee discussed the situation. "Our emphatic view is that the welfare of the animals must come first."

To encourage farmers to begin applying the new standards right away, the committee urged that grants once used to finance confinement methods, now be given to farms raising livestock in groups.

THE FUTURE OF ANIMAL MACHINES

All animals raised by factory-farming methods live and die under stress. Many of them never see daylight, trot through an open field, or nuzzle their fellow creatures. To control the boredom and stress which results from being raised in this unnatural way, workers confine, chain, push, prod, and medicate them.

For example, chemicals and other antibiotics, not currently against the law, are mixed liberally in their feed. And to save money, some factory farms even recycle ground up cardboard and manure in the feed.

One Chicago firm reported, in an article for *The Detroit News*, the tremendous savings one could expect by mixing the card-

Pregnant sows in confinement

board normally sent to the dump into dairy cattle feed. Little thought went into what effect it would have on the butter, milk, and cheese that eventually reached American tables.

And if that isn't savings enough, one can always run his hogs through the waste pits under the caged-layer factory. One Kansas farmer, in an article for *Hog Farm Management*, boasted that he saved $9,300 a year on feed by using this method with his pregnant sows.

On some farms, dirty litter from broiler houses is added directly to cattle feed. Other farms, less direct, mix poultry and pig manure with corn or shredded stalks before feeding it to the pigs.

THE EFFECT ON HUMAN HEALTH

According to a study done by the Animal Protection Institute of America, "The threat to human health (resulting from use of chemicals and antibiotics) is potentially serious, and the Federal Drug Administration wants to curtail their use; but the meat industry has become so dependent on drugs to fatten animals raised in concrete confinement systems that any regulating will be part of the distant future. Meanwhile, the public takes the risks and perhaps suffers the direct effects of these drugs."

In 1978, for example, one-eighth of the slaughtered pigs and milk from dairy cows in the United States contained illegally high levels of sulfa drugs.

RIGHTS AND WRONGS

The average American eats over six hundred pounds of animal products every year—twice as much protein as we need, according to the National Academy of Science.

Most of us, however, grow up on meat. We aren't really given a choice. It's part of the American tradition. And advertisers remind us of it every chance they get. What menu is complete without the all-American burger, Maine lobster, Southern fried chicken, New York cut steak, and sugar-cured ham from Iowa? And to most sports fans, no game would be the same without a foot-long hot dog or two!

This overconsumption of meat is one of our nation's greatest health threats. According to a report, *Healthy People,* issued by the Surgeon General of the United States, Americans need to decrease their intake of meat, heavy fats, whole milk, butterfat, and eggs.

Our addiction to animal protein also threatens the land and its wildlife. Livestock that are not being factory-farmed are overgrazing land meant to be the natural habitat of wildlife. And ranchers using federal land to graze livestock want government agencies to trap predators, such as coyotes and bobcats, and remove wild horses and burros from the public land they wish to use.

"Our demand for animal protein is also wasteful. Eighty percent of our corn, barley, and oats are fed to livestock," reports API, "which in turn is often grazed on land which could be used to raise crops."

Fortunately, many people are waking up to this terrible waste—a waste that threatens the well-being of humans as well as animals. And one that weakens the natural harmony and flow of the universe we depend on, as well.

GREENER PASTURES

Do we really have the right to force animals to live unnatural lives just to satisfy our unreasonable demand to eat huge amounts of their flesh?

This is a question more and more people are asking themselves and others, as factory-farming methods increase in our country and around the world.

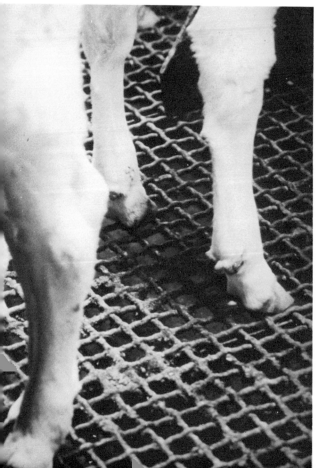

Foot and leg problems often develop from months of standing on wire-mesh surfaces.

For some, turning to vegetarianism—refraining from eating meat—is the answer. And the number of nonmeat eaters in our country is growing. According to the Vegetarian Information Service, a nonprofit educational organization, between 7 and 12 million people in the United States call themselves vegetarians.

Many people give up meat for health reasons as well as ethical reasons. Most say they just plain feel better and have more energy when they replace meat with more vegetables, fruits, and grains. To help people prepare nutritious and delicious menus, vegetarian cookbooks and restaurants specializing in nonmeat meals are also growing in popularity.

VEGETARIAN CELEBRITIES

Actress Carol Kane, known for her roles in *Hester Street*, *Annie Hall*, and the television series "Taxi," is a devout vegetarian. "There is no restaurant anywhere in the world where I have been," she reported recently, "that I haven't been able to find something to eat." Her favorite foods include baked potatoes with applesauce, chilies rellenos, vegetable tostadas, vegetable tempura, and all kinds of Chinese dishes made with tofu.

U.S. Representative Andrew Jacobs is also a vegetarian. And although his busy schedule includes many lunch meetings and formal dinners, he has had no problem avoiding meat. He simply eats ahead of time or spends the meal hour circulating through the crowd talking and shaking hands with people.

Violinist Yehudi Menuhin might be called a traveling vegetarian since he performs in cities all over the world. To meet his special food needs, he simply calls ahead and orders supplies from his favorite natural-food store. In New York, for example, he orders porridge, yogurt, goat's milk, sprouted wheat bread, ice cream, fruit, vegetables, tofu sandwiches, and kefir to be sent to his room.

Dennis Weaver, star of the television series "McCloud,"

originally became a vegetarian for ethical reasons. He objected to the killing of animals for food. Since then, however, he has also discovered the health benefits of a no-meat diet.

Weaver eats only two meals a day—usually salads of fruits or vegetables. Occasionally he will eat fish, when dining at a friend's home or in a restaurant where he is being interviewed. "No rule," he said, "should be so strong in our lives that it rules us. Every once in a while I break the rule just for that purpose."

Gwen Hutchinson, also a vegetarian, shared her views about raising animals for food. "I think people who do this (raise animals for food) are lying to themselves that it's 1983," she said. "There is so much information available now about how we don't need meat, that it's a lie to say otherwise. It's just not necessary." Millions of people live long, healthy lives without eating meat.

"There are also other ways to earn a living for people who now grow animals for food," Gwen continued. "I feel that if these farmers were supported in stopping all this, they'd find that they'd really rather do something else for a living."

The problem is that most of them are not supported financially or intellectually. If anything, farm and agricultural magazines and papers do just the opposite. They continue to splash expensive ads across their pages pushing the latest and greatest machinery, methods and money-saving techniques available to any farmer who wants to keep up with the times.

Can we ever hope to reverse the trend? Not unless we all get behind a campaign for massive education through television, newspapers, and journals. The government could also play an important role here. They could subsidize people to phase out meat and put something else in instead.

In Arkansas, for example, farmers were shown how to grow rice. It seemed an unlikely product for the area until they actually saw how ideal their soil is for this crop.

"All of this takes one showing another, trusting, and trans-ferring skills," says Gwen. "When people are supported in doing something they've never done before, they're more willing to give it a try. We already subsidize lots of things that don't make any sense (laboratory experiments on animals, for one), so why not switch to what does make sense."

Why not, indeed?

Chapter Five
Wildlife Endangered

The summer had been long and hot. The enthusiasm and promise of spring had drooped, along with the dark green leaves of the mimosa. Bright red and yellow zinnias had replaced the fragile whites and pinks of dogwood and rosebud. And now it was time to free the dove my brother had stolen from its nest in the wild orange tree.

Although I had fed the bird from time to time, I had never paid much attention to it as it hopped about the bottom of the old apple box my brother had converted into a cage. And I didn't really stop to examine it now as I reached into the cage, pulled the struggling bird out, and tossed it into the air.

Unprepared for this sudden freedom the young dove beat its wings frantically. Then it managed to fly to a small tree nearby where it scratched desperately at the limbs, then tumbled to the ground. Puzzled, I picked it up again and this time I paused to look at it. I was filled with dismay as I looked at the tiny, misshapen feet—twisted and distorted from months of walking on the bottom of the cage rather than curling around twigs and small branches. What had we done! My dismay was replaced by a great sadness. After several tries, I succeeded in getting the small crea-

ture to cling to a branch of the tree. And there I left it—
hopelessly unfit for the world outside its cage.

—Ray Hinchee

The buck pranced out from behind a small clump of scrub
pine, looking majestic and powerful under the unusually
warm autumn sun. He stood with his head high and nos-
trils flared as he surveyed the clearing for any signs of danger. He, of course, could not have known that this day was
to be his last, a final moment in what must be called a brief
existence.

My hands trembled as the moisture from my palms made
the rifle feel as if it were the culprit, and not the nervous
condition the locals called "buck fever." A moment later,
it occurred to me that I now had the power over life and
death. An explosion from the 308 and the feeling of power
faded as quickly as the buck that now bled beneath my feet.
I was suddenly helpless. I realized in that brief moment
that I could take a life if I wanted to, yet I could not give
one.

—Mike Brown

Both of these stories are true. The young boys involved,
however, are now men—Ray Hinchee, a school administrator,
and Mike Brown, an English teacher. I met both of them recently while I conducted a creative writing workshop for teachers in Houma, Louisiana.

I asked participants in the class to share on paper an incident
from their childhood that had made a deep and lasting impression on their lives. Afterwards volunteers read their work out
loud. Both Mr. Brown and Mr. Hinchee volunteered.

I was so moved by their stories, and the fact that these experiences were still fresh in their memories after so many years,
that I asked them if I could include their stories in this book.

Both men agreed, without hesitating.

FOREVER LOST?

Mr. Brown and Mr. Hinchee are not the only adults who have
learned from the mistakes of their youth. Most people seem to

have something in their past that they desperately wish had never occurred. And although we can't change what has happened, we can learn from it, as both admitted.

This is the very issue that wildlife defenders are talking about in regard to our nation's natural wildlife. The damage has been done. Hundreds of species are now extinct and hundreds more are threatened. What have we learned from our past mistakes? What are we going to do about this tragic waste before more animals are lost to us forever?

TIME IS RUNNING OUT

My desk is piled high with magazine articles, newspaper reports, brochures, letters, and posters—all saying the same thing in a different way. WHALING BAN THREATENED; RABBIT, RUN; THE FATE OF THE SEALS; HOW SAFE IS OUR WILDLIFE?; WILD HORSES IN PERIL. The list goes on.

"Time is running out for our endangered and threatened species," writes Attorney Michael J. Bean in an essay for *National Parks* magazine, July/August, 1983. "They are an irreplaceable gift that we must protect. Once they are lost we will

Fox caught in a trap

not have an opportunity to reconsider our folly. If they are to be preserved for our own welfare and that of future generations, we will need a commitment to a policy of good stewardship that is not transparent, but real."

What does it take? The task seems overwhelming. People don't agree on what stewardship is. People make laws, then break them. People get tired. People forget. People fight about what's right and wrong.

Meanwhile, seals, kangaroos, whales, wolves, coyotes, horses, rabbits, eagles, pelicans, and thousands of other animals lose their lives everyday because people don't have the time or the energy, the vision or the compassion, to discover ways to share the earth peacefully.

We are so full of "I want," "That's mine," "What's in it for me?" and "Just this once," that most of us don't even know how to simply appreciate another creature for what it is.

REFUGE OR DEATH TRAP

According to the September, 1983, *Close-Up*, newsletter of HSUS, there are currently 414 wildlife refuges of more than 86 million acres stretching from the Arctic to the Florida Keys and from Maine to American Samoa.

Most of these refuges have in some way been damaged by natural gas exploration, predator control, pesticides, and commercial farming, ranching, and lumber industries. And over one-half of all refuges are now open to hunting and trapping.

Regardless of the laws enacted "to preserve, protect, and enhance wildlife in its environment," refuges are now fast becoming dens of noise, pain, and death.

In 1982, for example, hunters killed 386,329 animals living on this nation's refuges. This number includes 219 swans and over 225,000 ducks. And the 85,473 mammals shot down included bobcats, mountain goats, majestic bighorn sheep, and tiny Sika deer.

Another twelve thousand animals were crippled and left to die from injuries, exposure, and starvation. From 1980 to 1983 alone, over half a million animals were trapped, mostly with the crushing leghold trap, which often causes a desperate animal to chew off its own leg.

NATIONAL DISGRACE

The cost to wildlife and the environment is tremendous. Pesticides, fuel exhaust, oil spills, and lead from used bullets poison the air, water, and plant life. And noise from jeeps, snowmobiles, airboats, drilling machinery, gunshots, and mining equipment frighten and drive away the animals from the very land that was set aside as their home.

Theodore Roosevelt established the first national wildlife refuge in 1903 when he realized that pelicans, herons, egrets, and other species would soon disappear if man continued to take a fancy to hats made with their feathers. Pelican Island became the nation's first wildlife refuge. But it wasn't long before the principles of preservation and protection which Roosevelt intended got set aside in favor of man's selfish interests.

In 1949, the federal government began opening refuges to hunters and trappers. More opened as years went on. Recently, however, the number has mushroomed. In the last five years, fourteen refuges were opened to trapping. And from 1981 to 1983, thirty-five opened to the hunting of one or more animals. Of the 220 open to hunting, 172 are home to endangered species.

The Fish and Wildlife Service has gradually backed down as hunters and trappers clamor for more openings. In fact, the FWS itself issued two statements which point out their views on the subject.

. . . The Service recognizes hunting [on refuges] as an acceptable and legitimate form of wildlife-oriented recreation . . . also, the listing of harvestable species should be expanded to coincide with State regulations where feasible . . .

. . . We believe that there is potential to expand economic uses in such areas as grazing, haying, farming, timber harvest, trapping . . .

In June of 1983, the HSUS gave formal notice that it will sue the U.S. Fish and Wildlife Service for violating the Endangered Species Act and the laws governing the National Wildlife Refuge System at Florida's Loxahatchee National Wildlife Refuge.

HSUS claims that if the FWS carries out its intention, Loxahatchee, one of the few remaining sections of the delicate Everglades, will be overrun with sport hunters in search of animal heads, pelts, and antlers for a trophy case, fur coat, or fireplace mantel.

According to the HSUS report, "This is the first time in the history of refuges that there has been an active and orchestrated push from the federal government to allow hunting and trapping on refuges."

As a result, the HSUS has expanded its wildlife protection program and has launched a major national campaign to protect the animals and their habitat.

WILD HORSES IN DANGER

Wild horses are no better off. Dr. and Mrs. Donald Molde, horse enthusiasts from Reno, Nevada, paid an unannounced visit to a Bureau of Land Management (BLM) wild horse roundup in 1982. They shared the results of their visit in a letter to the American Horse Protection Association and other humane groups.

The Moldes arrived at the trap site just as the helicopter was completing a sweep. They expected to see a large herd of wild horses being driven in, but instead were surprised to see a lone mare running toward the trap.

> Upon her arrival, the ground crew threw a noose around her neck and attempted to lead her to the corral. She was exhausted and fell to a sitting position, refusing to get up. One crew member twisted and pulled her tail, kicked her in the ribs, and cuffed her about the head. She was then dragged to her feet by a rider who pulled the noose tight about her neck. She skidded a few feet, collapsed, and the noose had to be loosened to allow her to breathe. Finally, she was forced into the corral.

As the couple continued watching, the helicopter completed another sweep and captured two more horses without effort. For an entire day's work, the roundup involved less than a dozen horses. The expenses were obviously great, the Moldes rea-

A Bureau of Land Management helicopter herds wild horses toward a capture trap.

soned. The BLM needed a helicopter at about $200 an hour, two men to operate it, three men in the ground crew, two BLM employees, several trucks, and a base camp including horses, feed, and so on.

Dr. and Mrs. Molde concluded that with a daily "take" of only a few horses, it's unlikely that the wild horse population is anywhere near the figure publicized by the BLM.

It appears that Nevada's wild horse problem, and perhaps those in other states as well, is nothing more than "a political windmill being tilted by taxpayers' dollars" because ranchers and certain political figures dislike wild horses.

PROJECT WILDLIFE

Aside from the work of large committed organizations, a number of other individuals like the Moldes contribute their love and energy to wildlife preservation on a day-to-day basis. Many spend their own money freely and share their homes and property openly with the injured and abandoned animals in their local communities.

Project Wildlife in San Diego County is one such group of people. I visited Martha Hall, director of the project, at her home and refuge in Alpine, California.

Martha, a schoolteacher by profession, and her husband, a fireman, became interested in wildlife conservation and habitat preservation, "which are terribly important," she emphasized, several years ago. "As we got involved with Sierra Club and the legal issues that affect wildlife," she said, sitting comfortably in her cozy, ranchstyle living room, "we kept coming across individual animals that were injured.

"Since, at that time, there was no agency or place to care for them in this area, they ended up with us." Then gesturing toward the yard, to her large brood of hawks, eagles, bobcat, young fox, baby raccoons, and resident deer, she added with a smile, "We never intended to have all that we now have."

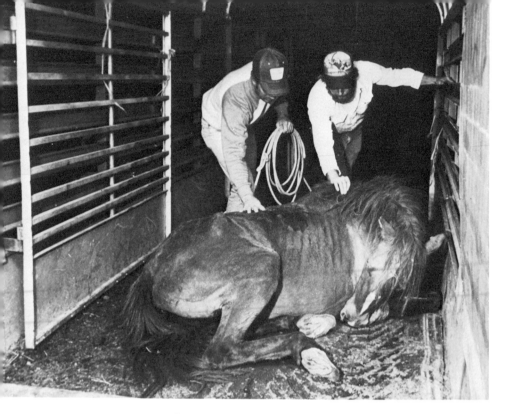

Humane workers assist an adopted horse found starving to death in Texas.

Martha stressed the fact that in her opinion, people make the greatest contribution if they spend their money on habitat preservation rather than caring for individual animals. "I feel strongly about this," she said, leaning forward in her chair.

"Project Wildlife cares for about two thousand animals," she explained, "and say we did return all of them to the wild, which of course we never do because most don't recover enough to go back, still that's nowhere near the number you could save if you could get another park set aside or a wilderness area, lagoon, or estuary."

Although Martha is not directly involved in habitat preservation right now due to a full teaching schedule, it is still her primary concern. And when people ask her how they can get involved, she always encourages them to work in this area.

She also feels that it's very important to become well-versed in the laws governing wildlife and how they work. For awhile Martha worked actively on the political/legal issues of wildlife preservation, but again, the irregular hours became difficult to manage while teaching full time.

"There are a few people in the Sierra Club who have the background for this," she explained, "and they are making a big contribution."

People seem to get involved caring for individual animals because, "Well—they're there," explained Martha, "and if you have a soft heart, it's hard to turn them away." Her large collection certainly reflects her soft heart. And, of course, many people (like Martha) just happen to like working with animals.

"Our group spends about $10,000 a year on food, medication, and some veterinary care," said Martha. "Beyond that, individuals spend whatever they want." Before the group organized eleven years ago, however, volunteers spent thousands of dollars of their own money.

Martha Hall cuddles baby raccoons.

As we strolled outside among the many homemade cages and animal enclosures, Martha continued to explain their work. "Although the Fish and Game Department, by law, has total jurisdiction over wildlife, they just don't have any place set up to handle them. So they are either left, taken to the Humane Society and destroyed, or individuals take them home and do what they can." Project Wildlife was organized to meet this need in the San Diego area.

A PLACE TO GIVE SOMETHING BACK

In some parts of the country animal welfare agencies and other groups have set aside land and facilities specifically for the rehabilitation of wildlife. However, most are still inadequate to the need, as more and more animals are injured and frightened out of their natural habitat.

In Monterey County, California, however, the Society for the Prevention of Cruelty to Animals (SPCA) recently opened their new George Whittell Wildlife Rehabilitation Center. This one-of-a-kind facility "is an ideal place to do work with native animals," said Martha.

Custom-built cages, aviaries, and a large veterinary hospital dot the graceful green grounds of this northern California stretch. As one of the opening day tour guides pointed out, most of the center's temporary residents are there because of man's encroachment on the wildlife habitat. The goal, of course, is to return its guests to the wild as soon as they are able.

Speakers during the opening ceremonies described the center as a place to "give a little something back" to the animals. Betty White, television actress and lifelong friend of animals, talked about what a special place it is. "This is the first time a wildlife rehabilitation center has been built from the ground up to accommodate all of the animal problems likely to be encountered in the community," she said.

The new operation will allow the wildlife staff to treat more

The George Whittell Wildlife Rehabilitation Center in Monterey, California

animals than ever before. In 1981, for example, before the center opened, they cared for two thousand animals.

The high point of the ceremony came when Pat Quinn, the director of the center, held up a kestrel that she had taken care of after it had collided with a car. With great enthusiasm she told the audience that she wanted to share with them the "unique feeling we have when we are able to release an animal that has been in our care." And with that, she released the bird to its rightful home in the wild.

HANDLE WITH CARE—AND LOVE

In San Diego, however, where such a facility does not exist, wild animals depend on compassionate individuals or groups such as Project Wildlife.

Martha explained that the injured or abandoned animals reach their members' homes in a variety of ways. "We pick up some.

Others are brought to us. Many referrals come from the Humane Society, the zoo, Animal Regulation Department, lifeguards, and so on," said Martha.

When members receive an injured animal, they can usually provide basic first aid. Most take care of simple wounds and small fractures without professional help. But if it's anything serious, they take the animal to a veterinarian. Martha quickly added that their group depends on several generous veterinarians who donate their time. "Without them we couldn't operate a group like this," she said.

Probably the most difficult thing to do after the animal has been treated is to design and set up appropriate cages and food programs for them. "A lot of the animals require special cages in order to survive in captivity," said Martha. "And we always try to give them food that is as close as possible to what they'd find in the wild."

To work in wildlife rehabilitation one needs some basic knowledge about how these animals survive in the wild, their natural habitat, and the food they eat. "I learned mostly from reading," said Martha, pointing to several of her books.

"When we started, however, very few people did what we do and there were not many books on the subject either. But in the last five to ten years all that has changed. There are a number of similar groups around the country and many good books, as well as a lot of dialogue between groups.

"The people in our group take animals according to their work schedule, preference, the type of home and yard they have, and so on," said Martha. One lady, for example, takes nothing but possums, another only hummingbirds.

"We never have enough people," added Martha, "especially for the very small animals that have to be fed every two or three hours around the clock. And we need a lot of people to take care of the hundreds and hundreds of baby songbirds that come to us every spring." To educate people on the care of these little creatures, the group sponsors a training seminar each year in April.

The work gets easier as the birds grow older. "Once they are self-feeding," said Martha, "they move into an aviary. We have about ten aviaries in our group. At that point, it's just a matter of putting out fresh food and water in the morning and evening."

Martha and her husband take the larger animals because they have the space to handle them. "At first, they're afraid of us," she explained, pointing out a suspicious looking hawk as we walked down the path behind her house. "But when they're injured we must handle them, so we move with caution, wear heavy gloves, and use a noose when it's necessary to give them shots or move them from one cage to another."

Each animal is released differently. Songbirds, for example, are let go directly from the aviary. "We feel it helps the animals adjust if we leave food in a place they can come back to, until they become adept at finding food in the wild. It's pretty

Martha Hall with baby fox

hard for hawks, eagles, and songbirds to get it all together in just a couple of days," Martha added playfully—"so we're kind of a halfway house at that point."

Deer and coyotes, on the other hand, remain with their keeper until the following spring when the fawns have their full size and the new grass is in. "One man allows us to release deer on his property," Martha explained. "He raises oat hay, so we wait until that's ripened before turning the animals loose."

WILDLIFE AND THE CITY FOLK

Much of the wildlife in San Diego is trapped by city people who find skunks, raccoons, fox, and possums in the open areas and canyons near their homes. "Sometimes the whole family can be relocated," said Martha, "sometimes not. We loan traps on a limited basis," she added, "but they're really not necessary. If people would just be willing to wait until the young grow up, the family would soon disappear." Most people aren't that patient, however. In fact, Martha finds most are rather intolerant of anything but their own pets.

Project Wildlife is working to educate people as much as possible to the needs of these animals. "We would like to see people become sensitive to them and let them eat a little of the fruit off their trees, and not come down so hard when they feel their pets are in danger. There are ways of managing pets so they will be safe from wildlife." But most people can't be bothered.

In fact, most of the calls their group receives are from irate pet owners who will do anything to protect their dog or cat. "They claim they 'love' animals," said Martha, "and they even have a poodle—with a nice name and a cute little collar and probably even a raincoat—to prove it."

Or they hear from angry cat owners who let their cats wander all night killing countless songbirds and whatever else they can find in the canyons. "Yet, if they think another predator might attack their cat or dog, they're ready to kill every coyote in San Diego County.

"The problem I notice regarding wildlife," she said, "is that so many people do not want to share any part of the earth with them. They think these animals should be put away in a park somewhere and that's the only place they should be allowed to exist."

She paused for a moment, then continued in a soft but certain voice. "But these animals have always lived in these areas, and I feel we should work out ways to share the land with them so we can both live."

Chapter Six
Behind Laboratory Doors

"Vivisection [experiments on live animals] is the only barbaric practice remaining from the dark ages," claims the National Antivivisection Society (NAVS). Thousands of people agree.

"Every second, three animals die in American laboratories. And up to one hundred million animals are sacrificed each year," according to statistics published by the Animal Protection Institute of America. In April, 1983, mass rallies took place throughout the world protesting the brutality, waste, and horror of the animal experimentation industry.

Every day intelligent primates, sociable rats and mice, friendly dogs, gentle rabbits, and other innocent animals lose their lives in the name of research. While still alive, many exist in crowded cages, often without the barest of essentials—medication, comfortable bedding, and bandages.

BREAKTHROUGH

A beautiful, intelligent monkey named Nero became such a victim in a laboratory in Silver Spring, Maryland. His treat-

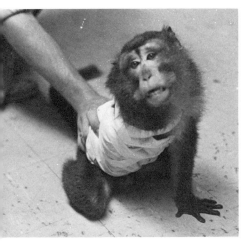

Nero, left, forced to use the arm where a nerve had been severed. His good arm is bandaged. Right: *Another of the Taub monkeys, Chester*

ment, unlike many others, however, did not go unnoticed. A technician in the lab took photographs and made careful notes about the conditions around him. He told authorities what he saw and knew, and a government investigation followed.

On Friday, July 2, 1982, following two-and-a-half weeks of testimony and careful review, a jury found Nero's keeper, Dr. Edward Taub, guilty of failing to give the monkey proper veterinary care. Taub's treatment of five other research monkeys at the same laboratory had been questioned the year before, but then overturned by a circuit court jury.

The story behind the trial began in May of 1981. Alex Pacheco, a part-time student at George Washington University and cofounder of a Washington, D.C., animal rights organization called People for the Ethical Treatment of Animals (PETA), applied for a job at Taub's laboratory, The Institute for Behavioral Research.

Pacheco told Dr. Taub that he wanted to get firsthand knowledge about how animal research laboratories work. Shortly

Alex Pacheco, cofounder of the organization People for the Ethical Treatment of Animals (PETA)

afterwards, Taub took him on as a volunteer.

Later that year, Pacheco testified at a government hearing on the treatment of laboratory animals. He talked in great detail about the work he was asked to do at IBR. His testimony appeared in an article for NAVS' *Bulletin* (Winter, 1982).

Within one week after he walked into the laboratory, without so much as an interview or questions about his experience or health, Pacheco received his first assignment.

> I was put in charge of a pilot study, assigned two primates in a separate room, and told to agitate and frustrate them and film their reactions. I asked the purpose of this study and was told, "It's never been done before. We might find something interesting, and if we do, we may get funding for it."

During this time, the young volunteer watched other researchers torment the animals, shake their cages, and tease and frustrate them with frightening noises. One even stuck a pair of surgical pliers between an animal's teeth while it was confined in a restraining device. Pacheco's "firsthand knowledge" came fast—and it sickened him.

> Meanwhile, the laboratory remained in an unchanged condition of extreme filth, disrepair, and disarray and the primates continued to be neglected in their barren cages. No occupied cage contained any bowl, resting board, or item of any kind for these intelligent, curious animals to manipulate. They used their lame arms as cushions to provide relief from the steel wire floors, and their own wounds and injuries as "things" to pick at and chew on.

Photographs included monkeys with open, unbandaged lesions on their arms, filth encrusted on the floor and cages, and a poorly functioning refrigerator, holding rotting food and outdated medication.

Dr. Taub's case was unique in the history of animal welfare. It was the first time a medical researcher had been successfully brought to trial under a state's anticruelty laws. It was also the first time the National Institute of Health (NIH) withdrew their funding (support money) because of the way a research animal was treated.

THE PRICE OF BEAUTY

Painful experiments with uncertain results take place in the cosmetic industry, as well. Products include toothpaste, shampoo, mouthwash, hand lotion, lipstick, face creams, eye cosmetics, hair conditioners, perfumes, and colognes.

One of the most appalling experiments is the LD/50 (Lethal Dosage Test). The purpose of the experiment is to see how large a dose of any given product would result in death for 50 percent of the animals tested.

To carry out the tests, the substances are forced on the animals—usually rabbits—through a stomach tube, in capsules, or mixed with their food. Reactions include gasping, loss of appetite, vomiting, diarrhea, abnormal posture, and a change in the condition of their coat.

Another bizarre experiment, the Draize test, involves testing cosmetics for eye damage. For example, researchers smear mascara or other eye products over the eyeballs of rabbits. Unlike humans, these animals have no tear glands to wash it off. This test is supposed to determine what effects the cosmetics will have on humans when it is applied around the eye.

Throughout the test, the animals are kept still in a stockade device. In some situations, their eyes are held open with clips. As a result, they cannot blink to get even a moment's relief. In the end many rabbits suffer from eye ulcers, bleeding, and blindness. And for what purpose? The tests don't even resemble the way in which humans would use the product.

DO ANIMAL TESTS PROTECT PEOPLE?

Despite the intense suffering of research animals, the only *real* test of a product's safety, however, comes from the people who use it. The cosmetic industry is not required to report customer complaints to the government. In 1970, however, the National Commission on Product Safety estimated that sixty thousand people suffer injuries from various cosmetics each year.

Then, in 1975, the Federal Drug Administration reported the results of a consumer survey they conducted. Their figures, including an estimate of people who don't bother to report their injuries, came closer to 2 million.

Torturous tests on animals that still result in injury and illness to humans are of little comfort to those people who thought they were buying a product that had been judged safe!

As philosopher Peter Singer discusses in his book *Animal Liberation*, either the animals are not like us, and if so, then there's no reason to perform the experiment, or they are like

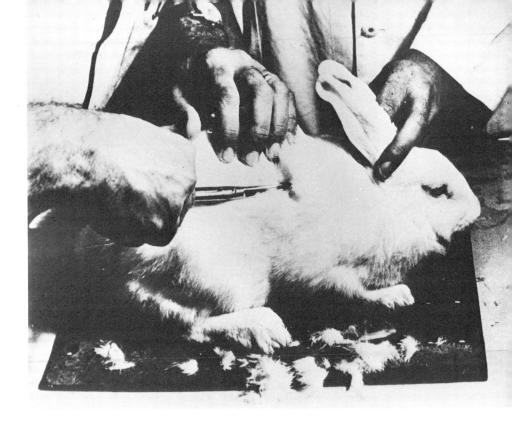

Clipping the fur of a rabbit before testing a chemical substance on the naked skin

us, and if so, how can we perform experiments on them that we would never agree to have performed on one of us.

So the next time you read or hear statements or claims such as, "The relevance of animal research findings to humans has not been established," or "Drawing comparisons between animals and people can be extremely misleading," or "Lethal doses in animals do not constitute lethal doses in humans," look and listen again. Don't they actually strengthen the stand against animal experiments?

PEOPLE TALK BACK

One man who stands firm on this issue is Steve Kowit, poet and university instructor from San Diego, who recently founded an activist group called Animal Rights Coalition.

Members of the local group are committed to fighting for new animal protection laws on the local, state, and federal levels. "We are part of a very fast-growing movement in the United States," Steve told me as we sat in the living room of his San Diego home where he lives with his wife, Mary, and assorted cats.

The animal rights movement, as Steve sees it, includes three different kinds of groups. "Liberationists," he explained, "are people who go into labs and actually take the animals out of their cages and set them free. Animal rights groups, on the other hand, study the issues involved. They look at how we treat animals in general within the culture. And they organize protests and campaigns for change. The animal welfare people more or less accept the way things are. But they do what they can to protect and minister to individual animals.

Steve Kowit, founder of the Animal Rights Coalition in San Diego

"To bring about change, you need all three," added Steve.

He continued, "Politically speaking, when people take to the streets and start demonstrating to get what they want, it reaches the media." News like this raises awareness, and gets people thinking and talking in a new way. "That level of achievement is blossoming in the United States today and we're part of it," Steve added, settling more comfortably into his chair.

FIRSTHAND EXPERIENCE

The Animal Rights Coalition has done a great deal to protest pound seizure and the use of animals in research. One of the group's most significant projects involved gathering sworn testimony from student technicians who have worked in the animal research laboratory at the University of California, San Diego (UCSD).

"If you want money for research," Steve explained, "you go into heart or cancer research. UCSD does a lot of both. The problem is," he continued, "most surveys show that 60 percent of what goes on in most labs is totally irrelevant. It's either been done before, is of no immediate value, or is so minor that it isn't worth the time and expense it required. Even if it's successful," Steve pointed out, "so many of the results don't really give us worthwhile knowledge about human beings."

Next, he talked about the scientists themselves, as he stroked a lone cat that had jumped onto his lap. "Most of them grew up in animal work. They've been told this is the only way to do reliable research. Animals are cheap and it's the only technology they know. These people are not experts in retooling—trying something new. Their beliefs were set years ago."

To illustrate some of the problems he talked about, Steve let me read and use the testimony of two of the student lab technicians. Following are their accounts of some of the things they saw and took part in.

"In general there was a lot of neglect," said Jan Rawlins, who

97

began work at UCSD as a caretaker assistant in 1978. (She had moved up to animal technician by the time she left in July of 1979.) "Dogs, for example, caught their toes in poorly designed cages or knocked over their water bowls during the night or on weekends and would then go without water for almost sixteen hours. That was fairly common," she added. "And these were dogs recovering from surgery, really critical ones. You could see how thirsty they were when they drank their water in the morning.

"I remember at least five different times when dogs came back from heart surgery and they'd have huge incisions. By the next day you could see whether or not they were going to make it. I'd try all day to get someone to look at them. 'Please someone, come. Otherwise the dog is going to die.' 'Okay,' they'd say, 'tell us when he dies.' Nothing was ever done. I'd come in the next day and there'd be two dead dogs, three dead dogs, dead dogs everywhere."

Next, Jan went to the researcher who had designed the project. "But no one in animal resources wanted to do anything either," she said. "It cost money."

Jan also felt that most of the people who worked in the lab didn't really care about animals. Of course, there were some who did, but to many it was just another job. "They cleaned up and kept quiet. And when I wanted to do extra things for the dogs, my supervisor told me not to do them because then everyone would want extras and we weren't being paid for that."

Jan felt that because she complained the most, certain workers had it in for her. One day she was ordered to break the necks of thirty mice. A technician told her that the gas machine (used to euthanize the animals) was broken. "I had to break their necks with a pen. It was a most incredible thing to experience. And the guys just stood there making jokes the entire time." Later, Jan found out the gas machine had not been broken after all. "That was the breaking point for me," she said.

ANOTHER VIEWPOINT

Patty McElhiney also worked as a technician at UCSD for three years and left in 1979. "I made several complaints during my time there," said Patty. "Mainly, they concerned the research animals—no one wanting to be responsible for their care."

The dogs were never exercised, according to Patty and Jan, never seemed to have enough water, and no one bothered to update their health reports. Patty entered something on a chart and nothing would follow it for days or weeks at a time. "In the meantime, animals had died and there was no mention of it."

Patty also talked about how she helped extend one experiment without realizing it. "One researcher got dogs to a certain point and they would stop eating. They would just die. I'd get down on my hands and knees and feed them until they got their appetites back. I was actually told that I helped extend the research."

The experiment needed to continue in order to get certain information. "But it had never gone that far before and they couldn't figure out why. They never realized that the animals had feelings, and that if they weren't eating, maybe it was more than the medication that was bothering them."

According to Patty and Jan most decisions seemed to be based on money. For example, technicians weren't allowed to give the animals shots or medication on weekends because they'd have to charge the researcher for their services. No one wanted to pay for that. "They could give the shots and medication themselves," said Patty, "but most of them didn't want to come in on weekends.

"Once I was holding [restraining] some rabbits for one of the vets," explained Patty, "and it seemed to me he was taking a lot of blood." She asked him what he was doing and he told her he was "bleeding them to death."

"These rabbits were conscious and I just held onto them," she said. "The needle took a long time going in. The animal would start to squeal and fight and I'd just have to hang on to him. They were in terror. It was incredible. Why didn't he order ten rabbits and take X amount of blood from each one? But this was a cheaper way to do it. They wouldn't have to pay the daily fee for each one anymore."

They saved money on rodents too, according to Patty. "A medium-sized rat box would hold three large rats. But they'd put as many as seven in them to save money because they were charged daily keep for each box."

Another time Patty was told to kill 120 rats that had been allowed to sit too long before an experiment. They had gained too much weight and had become too expensive to keep.

"I had to take them into surgery and euthanize them one at a time. I was gassing each one and by the time I got to the bottom of the cage they were frantic."

Patty made a final point. "I do believe in research," she said. "I do believe in using animals. But I believe there are certain guidelines and attitudes and procedures that have to be followed. They were not there, at least not when I left. At the time, I thought to myself I really should tell somebody about this, but there was nobody to tell."

A RESEARCHER SPEAKS UP

While gathering material for this chapter I also had an opportunity to go to UCSD and talk with one of the researchers and one of the doctors.

As I sat across from Frank White, senior researcher with the department of pathology, he began to explain his work—work he is obviously interested in.

"Our research has to do with the heart and how it's affected by certain diseases such as heart attacks. One of the things we've done for many years in the medical field is use animal models to mimic certain human diseases. The dog was the preferred

Researcher Frank White (left) and assistants at the University of California, San Diego, doing cardiovascular research on pigs.

model for most of the work," he said, "and it still is in many cases."

But after working with dogs for some time, the research team decided that dogs were no longer as appropriate as they had been. "For one thing," said Frank, "there aren't as many dogs available. Some of them come from the pound. They've been somebody's pet. They're pettable and friendly and this does make them easier and more fun to work with," he added, "but still many people feel this is not the thing to do."

Frank paused a minute, then added, "People don't seem to object to the use of pigs as much as dogs. Personally, I don't care to use primates either," he said. "I feel bad using any animal that comes from the wild. But to me, a pig is like a cow or anything else we raise for research."

Frank explained that a pig's heart is close in size and dimension to a human heart and that its diet can also be made to resemble a human diet. Pigs are also very easily exercised, so they seem to work out well for the studies done on the treadmill.

When I asked Frank how the pigs take to running, he said, "I wouldn't say they enjoy it, but then I run every day and I'm not sure I enjoy it!"

Overall, claimed Frank, "They approach exercise a lot like humans. They'd rather take it easy, lie quietly in the shade, and eat as much as possible."

Next, Frank talked about what it's like to actually work with the pigs. "We know when a pig is tired and when he's pretending to be tired," said Frank. "There are lots of little ways to communicate with them. In fact, some people feel they have a language of their own," he added. Then pausing for a moment,

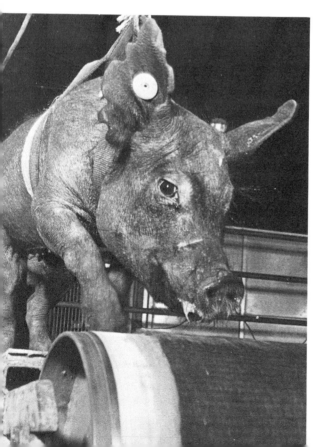

One of the pigs used in the UCSD School of Medicine cardiovascular study

he said, "I wouldn't be a bit surprised. They do seem to communicate. On the treadmill, for example, you can tell by their grunts what level of stress they're at."

The research team has spent the last six or seven years training pigs to run on treadmills. They may run one day a week or every day, depending on the studies.

"We've done more thoracic [heart and lung] surgery than anyone else in the world, and we will continue for at least five more years," said Frank. "We intend to show the relationship between exercise and heart disease—how exercise works, how much, if it's good for people, and whether or not you can still exercise if you have heart disease. We also want to introduce a lot more people to the pig. It's easily available, not too expensive, and quite appropriate."

How do they conduct these studies? Frank continued to explain their work. "We do experiments in which we give the pig a small heart attack. For the most part, I don't think they even know they've had one. They don't seem to show pain, at least in the same way humans do."

Then he added quickly, "Certainly if you stick a pig with a pin he's going to squeal and jump like you or I would, but where the heart is concerned they don't seem to show the same response. We don't understand this so far."

"How many pigs do you use and how long do you keep them?" I asked.

"We keep them about a year at the longest," he answered. "All the pigs eventually get autopsied [examined and dissected after death]. We go in and take the heart and examine it in great detail. In the end all the pigs go the same way. We euthanize them."

I asked Frank if he ever feels attached to the pigs. "Oh sure I do," he said. "But you have to learn in this business that at a certain point in time you just don't think about it.

"I know I've been featured on the Humane Society's 'black

list'," said Frank, "and I can see why from their point of view. My daughter belongs to the Humane Society and she doesn't like the work I do either.

"I use about fifty pigs a year," said Frank, turning the conversation back to his current work. "One a week on the average. That's sufficient to keep us busy cranking out reams of data. In fact, we're publishing a paper right now on how exercise at the right time following a heart attack has a saving effect on the heart." Then Frank added, "But it's also rather tricky to determine how much exercise since everyone is different."

Frank agreed that it would be better if these studies could be done on humans. "But they can't," he said. "Most of us don't want anything done to us, let alone someone sticking gadgets in our hearts and making us run on treadmills."

I thought about the pigs. I wondered how they felt about it.

It was as though Frank read my thoughts because his voice softened for a moment and then he said, "I think that if we really thought about it from the pig's standpoint, we simply couldn't do the work."

"What about the work Nathan Pritikin does in the field of heart research?" I asked. "He works directly with human beings and he's had amazing results with heart attack victims by changing their diet and setting up a special exercise program."

"He's not widely accepted by the medical profession," said Frank. "Some people think he's a bit, well, strange. Actually we're trying to get information here that supports what he does."

Next, Frank talked briefly about the support money they receive for the work they do. "There is a kind of policing system built into the research grants," he explained. "Money is so hard to get that if you're not out there showing new ways of doing things, you're not going to get funded."

Then Frank talked about the demands of his job. "I feel like I'm at war all the time. There's never a day when I'm not on the firing line. I have no guarantee of a single dollar coming my way beyond what I can prove is a good idea and then do it."

If the work is so stressful, why does Frank stay in the business? I really wanted to know. "If I could get the knowledge out of a little box I'd prefer to do it that way," he said. "This is difficult and sometimes impossible work, but it's the very impossibility that pushes me on."

And how does Frank feel about all the publicity and protest going on from animal rights groups? "They're assuming animals have feelings and intelligence like mine and I'm assuming they don't," he answered matter-of-factly. Then he added quickly, "And I don't think any of us knows for sure. We really don't know. Anyway, my favorite response to that question is 'Do you eat meat?' If the person says, 'No, I'm a pure vegetarian,' then I say, 'You've got a good point.' To me that's the bottom line."

A DOCTOR SPEAKS UP

Frank White prepared me for my next meeting. "Wait till you meet Colin," he said, as I walked to the door. "Now there's a compassionate man. Some of the people around here don't really care, but we've worked together for fifteen years, and I can tell you he really cares."

Within minutes I was seated across the hall in Dr. Colin Bloor's compact office. I asked Dr. Bloor to talk about his work in heart research and how animals are used.

"Animal models are used in research in a number of ways," he began in a soft, friendly voice. "We induce disease in some of them," he said. "We put certain instruments in the animals and then watch them over a period of time to see what takes place. This helps us find out what we need to do to correct or prevent the disease in humans. We most frequently use that type of animal model here.

"Another type would be a dog or other animal with a naturally occurring disease. For example, a dog breeder contacted us about his show dogs that had heart disease. This gave us a

Dr. Colin Bloor with one of the pigs used for research at UCSD

chance to study a group of animals that had a disease that is probably the closest to what occurs in humans."

Other ways to use animals, Dr. Bloor explained, include toxicology—looking at new drugs and testing compounds for safety. "I feel some changes could be made here," he said. "Some people want to replace animals with computer models. This can be done to a large extent. But since they are modeling information from the biological system, it's important to keep in mind that nature and biology are still unpredictable."

I asked Dr. Bloor if he ever gets personally involved with the pigs. "Of course you get attached," he said. "And you notice different personalities." He chuckled a moment, then continued. "In fact, the daughter of one of our staff took one of the pigs home at a week of age and trained it to run with her Great Dane. The pig could even be let off the leash and it kept up with the dog."

Dr. Bloor also mentioned that he feels it's important to separate one's feelings when certain procedures have to be done. You have to be realistic about the work.

"My purposes for doing this work," he said, "is to try to answer a series of unending and challenging questions, and to help young people get started in research. It's personally rewarding," he said, "to help new doctors develop their careers."

DOWN ON THE PIG FARM

After talking with Frank White and Dr. Bloor, I visited the training grounds, sometimes called the "pig farm," where the pigs live and train.

One afternoon I had an opportunity to watch one of the pigs training on the treadmill and then to talk to the trainer. "We put the pigs through an intense training program," said Abby Waltz, a trim, attractive college student who is considering becoming a veterinarian. "It is not one you'd want to put yourself on. But it is probably the most efficient use of the time we have."

Abby, a runner herself and also an aerobic dance instructor, talked about her work with the pigs. "We run stress tests here," she said, "to determine how heart rates respond to a certain work load put on them."

One of the biggest challenges, according to Abby, is "knowing how long and how hard to push the pigs. You have to be sensitive to their bad days," she said, patting the fat dark pig on the treadmill in front of us. "At the same time," she continued, "we have to get the work done. I need to keep a balance."

Abby said that before she took the job she did "give some thought to the fact that all the animals are done away with after

Trainer Abby Waltz observing one of her charges at the UCSD "pig farm" near San Diego.

the experiment is over. And yet," she added, "there aren't too many things in medicine that haven't been tried on animals first. But I don't believe in abusing them," she said strongly.

"Who's right and who's wrong?" she asked. "Well, it seems nobody wants to get their hands dirty, and yet those who are against using animals in research often have a friend or relative who had a successful treatment or surgery that was probably done on an animal first. As I said before, I don't believe in abusing them."

"What do you think of as abuse?" I asked her.

"Well, if I notice that a pig is tired and continually hitting the shocker [a device to keep them going], then I know that's enough for that day. It's not doing the animal or me any good.

At that point, the pig starts to break down instead of producing results."

Next, Abby showed me the cages where the pigs are housed. Then she talked briefly about her relationship with them. She has given most of them names. In fact, one she named Abby.

"They definitely show a personality," she said, "and I enjoy them, but it's also important for me to put things in perspective." She looked away for a moment, then added, "If there was another way of getting the same results, I'd be all for it."

LOOKING WITHIN

After talking with these people, and reading reams of material on animal research, I see that there isn't one of them—or anyone on earth, for that matter—who wouldn't be in favor of healing disease, easing the stress of everyday living, and doing whatever we can to improve the quality of life.

But how do we find the answers to these challenges? I can't help but feel we are looking in the wrong place for our answers. For the most part, we're still trying to solve today's problems with yesterday's methods. And it just doesn't work. Animals aren't the only creatures in pain. The people who inflict the pain suffer too. And so do all of us who stand by and watch.

We can only grow as human beings when we reach out in love to all of life—when we look deep within our own hearts for the answers we seek—when we are willing to listen to that part of us that knows, absolutely, that if even one creature suffers, we all suffer.

As the famous author, philosopher, and humanitarian George Bernard Shaw wrote many years ago, "You do not settle whether an experiment is justified or not by merely showing that it is of some use. The distinction is not between useful and useless experiments, but between barbarous and civilized behavior. Vivisection is a social evil because if it advances human knowledge, it does so at the expense of human character."

Chapter Seven
New Age Research

"Your patient has just died of irreversible shock," spelled the announcement. The attending doctor is disappointed by the news but not discouraged, because he knows that within minutes he can revive the body and begin treatment again.

How can this be? Well, fortunately, the "victim" is a computer patient, and the "doctor" a medical student sitting at a computer terminal where he is learning how to treat a car accident victim.

This report from a newspaper article in the *Sudbury Star*, Canada, April 15, 1974, is just one example of the many amazing research alternatives that have come about during the past ten years.

Allowing students to "kill" their patients then revive them and start again appears to be an effective way to teach and learn. Students also learn about heart disease in a specially designed cardiology program at the University of Alberta in Edmonton.

Twenty-one computer terminals are used. Each one is equipped with a television-like screen giving students a picture

Computer testing at the University of Alberta, Canada

Medical student at computer terminal

of the human body, some printed materials, an image projector supplying x-rays, and an audio unit which mimics the heart-beat.

Students receive the patient's symptoms and family history. Then they indicate the necessary treatment by typing on a keyboard or using a light-sensitive pen.

The cardiology program includes nine "patients" with different heart diseases, several test cases, and a multiple-choice examination. Students like the course because it allows them to work at their own speed. They're in control and "don't have to tag along behind a doctor," said medical program analyst Wayne Osbaldeston.

The program does not substitute for medical training. It is combined with lectures, seminars, and work in hospital wards. Personal feedback seems to be one of its most popular features. The computer keeps track of how many correct responses a student makes, then gives a printout of his/her performance. Students are then able to see and correct their problems, if any, before they fail the course.

EVERYTHING BUT PAIN

Human-acting robots are also being used in a number of research areas. According to a report by the National Antivivisection Society, "They bleed when cut. They react when hurt. They have a heartbeat, they breathe, they even cough and vomit. They react to injected anesthesia. The pupils of their eyes contract and dilate in response to certain conditions. And they don't hurt a bit."

Another similar device trains dentists. It jerks its head when a drill strikes a "nerve" and it even says "ouch." It salivates, has a tongue that gets in the way of instruments, and gums that can swell. And the dentist can quickly replace its teeth when necessary.

WHY ANIMAL TESTS?

If these techniques are now available and more are being discovered each year, then why do we continue to use animals for testing?

One reason has to do with peoples' *attitudes*. Most people, for example, are surprised and shocked to find out what goes on behind laboratory doors. They had no idea that animals suffered and died as a result of tests. But then after the first reaction dies down, they forget about it or assume that it's just a fact of life—something we have to put up with if medicine and science are to advance.

On the other hand, some people are so angry and outraged they demand an immediate end to all animal research. They campaign against the cruel treatment, write letters to their congressmen, and some even go in and set the animals free.

Others feel that using animals for some experiments may still be necessary. So they work to get laws passed which will protect the animals from abuse during research. And still others feel that the way to make progress without pain is to look for alternatives, methods of doing research that would not require the use of live animals.

The attitude of scientists is perhaps even more crucial than the average citizen because they are the ones who are actually doing the work. Many of them, for example, regard research animals as "tools" or "models," not as living creatures that can feel pain. As a result, they don't see any need to rush out and replace them with computers or robots or mathematical programs.

Others continue with animal research because it's a career they have developed over a long time. They don't want to give up the security or the recognition that goes with the job.

In other cases, union workers and large companies that sell to the public are afraid to step out and try something new. An-

113

imals are cheap, they have relied on animal tests in the past, and they want to continue to do what they know and understand.

Still others are afraid of being sued if a product fails or causes injury or illness. To say that the product was first tested on animals is a good defense.

But none of these reasons holds up when we look at the countless number of innocent animals that suffer and die each year in the name of science.

NEW DIRECTIONS

Pain and death are not the answer. Killing never spells progress. Alternatives are always available—if we have enough desire and commitment to find and use them. The airplane, telephone, radio, television, automobile, and many other inventions came about just this way.

No one is stuck with worn-out ideas or methods as long as we have imagination. Many people—maybe even most people—however, are afraid to try anything new, no matter what it is. The first fear that comes up is survival. How will it affect me? Will it work? What if I fail? What will people think? Most of us are more comfortable doing what we know and what we are good at.

In order to succeed and advance, however, you don't necessarily have to give anything up. It may simply require using a familiar talent or skill in a new way. And when people can see how this could apply to their own lives, they are usually more willing to give it a try.

For example, scientists who regard research animals as tools could just as easily replace them with modern, less expensive, more accurate nonanimal "tools." They would not need to give up their lifelong work—just move in a new direction. They could still continue their research and publish their findings just as they do now.

Researchers who are concerned about job security could choose, instead of working with animals, to work in nonanimal research, and still earn a living as well as recognition. Many organizations and companies are now offering grants for alternative research.

Overall, nonanimal methods are also less expensive than raising and housing thousands of animals each year. Cages, food, veterinary care, and salaries and offices for caretakers and technicians would no longer be necessary.

Companies that are afraid of lawsuits could focus their money and energy on alternative methods that would actually reduce the number of injuries (and lawsuits) each year, especially since animal tests are often unreliable and inaccurate when applied to human problems.

OTHER NONANIMAL METHODS

As people become interested and committed to alternatives, more ideas and more money for research seem to appear. It is amazing what we can produce when we want something strongly enough.

The following examples are just some of the exciting and significant new alternatives to animal research. Some are in use right now. Others are being developed and tested for future use.

The list includes material furnished by the American Fund for Alternatives to Animal Research (AFAAR) in New York and The Lord Dowding Fund for Humane Research in England.

Cell Cultures—Individual cells can be kept "alive" in the laboratory for specific periods of time, easily seen and counted. And the effects of added drugs, hormones, and other chemicals which change their shape and growth can be measured. By using cultures, scientists have successfully detected viruses, come up with vaccines to combat viral infections, and created antibiotics.

Since all animal disease and responses to foreign chemicals

Parts of three teams of scientists working with AFAAR to develop nonanimal replacements.

start at the cell level, this approach is practical as well as humane.

The Draize Replacement—Dr. Joseph Leighton of the Medical College of Pennsylvania has discovered that the chicken-egg membrane (chorioallantoic membrane) can substitute for live rabbits in the Draize test (where chemicals such as oven cleaners and eye cosmetics are poured into the naked eye).

This test involves several steps over a period of weeks. First, the scientist holds the egg in front of a light so he can see the blood vessels. Next, he cuts a small window in the shell and covers it with tape. Later the tape is opened and a plastic ring is used to hold the membrane while he inserts the test material. When the membrane responds to the injury, the researcher then studies the changes and records them. This test involves no pain, since the nine-day-old chick embryo does not have sensory nerve fibers.

Scientists at Colgate-Palmolive have been so impressed with results, that the company has offered Dr. Leighton a research grant to continue and speed up his work.

Ethel Thurston, Ph.D., of AFAAR, one of the organizations that helped fund Dr. Leighton's work, told the National Anti-vivisection Society that "several prominent scientists" claimed that "of all the Draize test alternatives being investigated, Leighton's approach appears to have the edge."

Reducing LD-50—Replacements for this dreaded test have also been slow to appear, but change is beginning to surface. For example, scientists, toxicologists, even the cosmetics industry itself have finally offered support for finding alternatives. Revlon, Bristol-Myers, the Cosmetic, Toiletry & Fragrance Association, Estee Lauder, and others have provided grant money for nonanimal testing research.

This shift in the wind is largely the result of a growing movement, Coalition to Stop Draize and LD-50, coordinated by Henry Spira. The Coalition represents more than four hundred animal welfare societies.

As more nonanimal research programs are funded, Mr. Spira expects even more progress to be made toward the Coalition's goal of eliminating animals from laboratories. The Coalition is

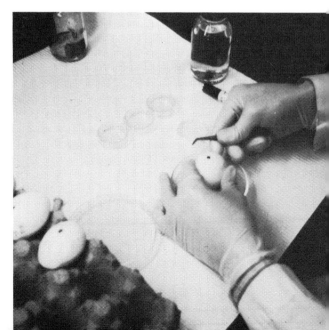

Chick embryo skin replacing hamsters and mice to test substances for cancer. Research is supported by AFAAR and the Lord Dowding Fund.

also asking cosmetics firms to support nonanimal research at institutions across the country.

Organizations outside the cosmetics industry have also provided support for new research. For example, AFAAR and its parent society, The Lord Dowding Fund for Humane Research in London, offer yearly grants to scientists in their search for nonanimal alternatives and experimental techniques. Their purposes are to:

1. save thousands of animals from painful tests

2. provide opportunities for researchers to develop new alternatives

3. put pressure on government agencies to use more funds for developing nonanimal research.

So far, results have been very encouraging. In addition to Dr. Leighton's significant work, Dr. John Petricciani conducted research in human muscle tissue under a grant from AFAAR and The Lord Dowding Fund. As a result of his studies, it is now possible to use human muscle to show the difference between tumor and nontumor cells.

"This method," according to a report from AFAAR, "eliminates not only the need for live animals but even the need for animal tissues."

Just as important, Dr. Petricciani's work was recognized publicly. In 1982, he received the "Clinical Society Award" from the United States Public Health Service Professional Association.

This prize is important for two reasons. It is a special tribute to Dr. Petricciani personally. But it is also an example and encouragement to others who wish to enter the field of nonanimal research.

The Ames Test—Here is another test which shows what dedicated and imaginative researchers can do. This method uses bacteria to test whether chemicals can cause cancer. It takes only a few days to accomplish, is inexpensive, and very sensitive. It appears to be a welcome replacement for the traditional and expensive cancer test on animals which takes two to three years to complete.

Scientists can also test more chemicals using the Ames method than would be possible with animals. It cannot detect all dangerous compounds. Therefore, it is best used together with one or more of the many other alternatives.

The Human Placenta—One of the most interesting new possibilities is this versatile organ which is formed to nourish the fetus, then discharged after birth. It has some of the properties of the liver and can also produce enzymes and hormones. So far researchers have tested the placenta for the effects of aspirin and alcohol. Results look promising so they are now trying a larger variety of drugs.

Humane Screening Techniques—This alternative can provide clues to useful medicines. For example, researchers have discovered that mung beans might be helpful in developing drugs to treat epilepsy. So far they have classified eleven out of fourteen known drugs using this method.

Anticancer Drugs—Human cancer cells could be used to test new anticancer drugs. This approach also helps determine which currently known drugs are best for individual patients. Doctors remove some of each patient's cancer cells and then test them with a variety of known anticancer drugs. Those which don't work or have harmful side effects can then be avoided

Learning from Plants—Research now shows that plants can also develop cancer. By treating some plants with a bacterium, normal cells change into cancer cells. These tumors can be used to test chemicals for anticancer reactions. Recent research indicates that potatoes might be used in this way to replace the traditional tests using mice.

Safe and Effective Human Research—Regardless of the method, the safety of any drug cannot be truly known until it is tested on human volunteers. New techniques in this area, using small amounts of drugs or other chemicals, are being carried out safely and producing encouraging results.

For example, by using a tiny amount of radioactive chemical to mark the brain's active areas, and a brain scanner to locate the chemical, pictures are produced which show the brain in health and in disease. This technique can help researchers study stroke, epilepsy, Parkinson's disease, and others.

LABORATORY INSTRUCTION

New research is important. But equally important is educating and training premed students in the area of nonanimal research. AFAAR, in addition to providing research grants, also offers courses for college and high school students who are interested in a career in biology or medicine. The response has been exciting.

For example, their summer 1983 course, "Introduction to Tissue Culture and In Vitro [under glass] Toxicity Testing," drew so many students that AFAAR presented it twice instead of once, as originally planned.

DAWN OF A NEW AGE

Many of the alternatives mentioned above are still being developed and studied. Some are limited and incomplete. That is why education and people sharing their views and experiences with one another are so important. Early stages of research require time and patience—and faith that answers will come.

Other replacements, however, offer real hope for those of us who are anxious to see the end of animal suffering. In fact, many of the alternatives listed have already replaced or greatly reduced the number of animal victims.

We still have a long way to go. But change is in the air. Things are happening today that we had no knowledge of ten or twenty years ago. Attitudes are also beginning to change. Every day thousands of people, including scientists, are waking up to the responsibility each of us has to make this world a better place for all living creatures.

Chapter Eight
Sharing the Kingdom:
Students Speak Out

Susanne Strachan, a student at Agoura High School in Southern California, armed herself with the facts about animals used for research. She also gathered information about new research methods that do not require live animals. Next, she wrote directly to President Reagan about her concerns. And she included in her letter signatures from 817 of her fellow students.

A few weeks later Susanne received a personal reply from President Reagan encouraging her to continue to speak out for what she believes in.

In San Mateo, California, the Peninsula Humane Society started a club for young people. In less than a year, the Animal Kindness Club (AKC) had enrolled sixty members. The club is for students who want to do something to help animals in need. Members meet twice a month at their schools. Meetings include a wide variety of activities. They discuss current animal problems, look at films, play games, write letters, plan field trips, and talk about ways to raise money.

One way the students have been speaking out for animals is by writing letters to lawmakers regarding certain bills that affect how animals are treated. They also learn about various kinds of animals through field trips. They have visited Guide Dogs for the Blind to see how blind people learn to work with dogs. They've also taken a Whale Watch boat trip to see the annual migration of California gray whales.

Meanwhile on the other side of the country, junior high student and member of the Humane Society of the United States, Barbara Prigitano traveled to the Connecticut state capitol in the spring of 1983. As reported in *Kind News*, she told a committee of lawmakers that she agrees with a proposed law that would allow elderly people who live in special apartment houses to keep pets. Barbara understands the needs of these people, because as she told the committee, "I will be old someday and will want to be able to have a pet."

Animal Kindness Club of the Peninsula Humane Society of San Mateo, California

Barbara Prigitano speaking before lawmakers at the Connecticut State Capitol.

Barbara also organized a group at her school called We Care About Animals (WCAA). Members publish a newsletter sharing their concerns about animals with parents, teachers, and students in their community of Durham.

In the same state, according to a report in *Agenda* magazine, college student Laura Simon started a debate on animal experimentation among faculty and students at Wesleyan University in Middletown.

On April 17, 1983, around 10:00 P.M., Laura walked over to the college's biology lab. She had heard from other students that mice that had been used in an "aggression" experiment were still caged together and fighting. As Laura entered the lab she heard the squeaking mice and could see that several were still attacking one another. Two were bleeding and badly injured from tail-biting and chewed-up ears.

Laura separated the fighting mice and put them into other cages. Next she scratched a hurried note on the blackboard and took the two injured mice home. The note read, "We mice decided that we don't like being mangled and crowded so we moved elsewhere."

Next, Laura wrote a letter describing what she had found—crowded cages, injured and bloodied mice—then signed it along with a dozen other "supporters." Shortly afterwards, it appeared in the school newspaper, *The Argus*. Laura's letter, together with a series of interviews she conducted with professors on campus about animal experimentation, opened up this controversial topic.

Although not everyone agreed with Laura's action, she did receive several calls from instructors congratulating her on doing a fine job of shedding light on an important issue. Many students who shared Laura's views backed her up.

"I was surprised," said Laura, "at how many students told me that they, too, had felt uncomfortable or upset about having to do animal experimentation in science classes, yet felt that they were alone in their feelings." Most were also afraid to take a public stand until Laura set an example to follow.

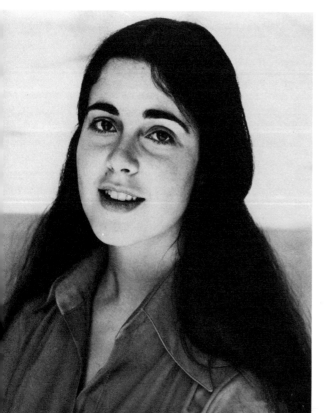

Laura Simon at Wesleyan University

Marlene Lakin

At the close of school in June, the issue of animal experimentation still seemed very much alive. In fact, it looked as though it would start up again in the fall. Two professors who supported Laura's action agreed to interview her for an article to appear in the school's alternative paper, *Hermes*, at the beginning of the next school term.

And across our northern border, Canadian Marlene Lakin, while still a teenager, learned from an article in a Toronto newspaper about the large number of animals being killed for food. Shortly afterwards, Marlene dedicated herself to working in the animal welfare movement. She became a vegetarian and joined every animal protection organization she could find.

Since then, she has become involved with the Farm Animal Reform Movement (FARM). She was one of the group's first and most active coordinators. And she has been very successful getting media attention for the cause of farm animals.

These are just a few of the many young people who have been actively working for the protection and welfare of animals. There is a place in the animal rights movement for everyone who is interested.

What can you do? And how can you get started? Following are some suggestions that might interest you and your friends. And if you care to write to any of the organizations mentioned, check the list at the back of the book for current addresses.

THE ANIMAL RIGHTS MOVEMENT

1. If you are interested in an overview of this growing movement and would like to arrange a group activity on the subject, write to the Animal Rights Network, Inc., for information and an order form regarding their twenty-minute slide presentation (on film with music and narration) titled "Animal Rights: The Issues, The Movement." This film is ideal for junior high and high school classes, Scouts, social, civic and church youth groups. It also comes with a list of activities and follow-up material for discussion.

2. Write to the Society for Animal Rights and request copies of their pamphlet, *10 Easy Ways to Be Kind*. This would make a good handout to share with members of your class, youth group, or club.

3. If you would like to read more about certain animal problems, write to the Animal Protection Institute and ask for their *Order Form for Materials*. They offer brochures, books, posters, bookmarks, information packets, and protest packets, many available free or for a small fee. Some of the titles include *Everyperson's Guide to Animal Rights*, *How to Become Actively Involved for Animals in Your Community*, and *The Pet Population Tragedy*.

4. Write to the various animal welfare and protection associations listed in the back of the book and request information about their services and activities. Join the ones that interest you. Participate in their programs. Many have divisions tailored for young people.

5. If you are interested in buying food, clothing, and cosmetics that are cruelty-free—in other words, those that do not

include any animal products—you can write for a special list of places to shop. Send for your copy of *The Compassionate Shopper* from:

Beauty Without Cruelty
175 West 12th Street (16G)
New York, NY 10011.

TEACHING PEOPLE ABOUT ANIMALS

There are many good educational programs available for use in schools and community groups. Sometimes teachers, librarians, Scout leaders, and parents are not aware that they exist. If you would like to see more children develop a healthy respect for all living creatures, as well as the environment, you might suggest some of these materials to the adults you know who work with young people.

1. The National Association for the Advancement of Humane Education (NAAHE) offers a special school program for students in preschool through sixth grade. This curriculum guide, called *People and Animals*, blends thirty-five humane concepts with the teaching of language arts, social studies, math, and health/science. The four general headings are called Human/Animal Relationships, Pet Animals, Wild Animals, and Farm Animals. This group also publishes a magazine for teachers called *Humane Education*. The publication provides informative articles, book reviews, and listings and announcements of educational materials available from a wide variety of sources. For more information, write to the NAAHE.

2. Write to other animal welfare groups on the list and ask about their educational materials. Then share these with your teachers and other adult friends.

HELPING DOMESTIC PETS

According to a 1983 report from the HSUS, "Up to 13 million animals must suffer an early death in the United States be-

127

cause they do not have a home." But solving this problem is no mystery, they claim. If everyone followed their "blueprint for successful pet overpopulation control," this vast amount of suffering would stop.

1. Talk to your government officials. Write to your lawmakers and urge them to pass laws that would require pet owners to spay and neuter their animals. And let them know how important it is to sponsor humane education programs. Share materials you have so they can see the numbers for themselves.

2. Help inform your family, friends, neighbors, and relatives. Write to the HSUS for details about their posters, ads, and pamphlets that describe the importance of responsible pet ownership. You might want to order some yourself and share them with people at school, libraries, movie theaters, and supermarkets.

3. Spay and neuter your own pets. Regardless of whether or not you find homes for them, every newborn puppy or kitten adds to the problem of overpopulation.

4. Be sure your pets wear identification tags. This can reduce their chances of ending up in a lab.

ANIMALS IN ENTERTAINMENT

1. Write to the American Humane Association and inquire about their film listings. Find out how you can let producers know that you do not support movies that injure or deprive animal actors of humane treatment.

2. Do not attend rodeos, bullfights, dog and horse races. Every dollar you spend at one of these events helps to continue the exploitation of animals.

3. Encourage your school to sponsor animal fairs that educate students as well as entertain. Depending on where you live, perhaps your class could schedule field trips as the Animal Kindness Club did.

4. When you visit the zoo, do not tease or feed, heckle or

pester the animals. And if you see other people doing these things, take a stand for animals. Go up and remind them politely that the animals are special and they deserve to be treated with care.

It would seem that everyone knows better than to mistreat the animals, but it's just not true. A monkey at the San Diego Zoo, for example, choked to death on a paper clip. An ostrich died when a flashcube caught in its throat. And a deer died after eating a balloon and a plastic bag in the Children's Zoo.

5. Keep in mind that true entertainment does not rely on cruelty to animals.

ANIMALS FOR FOOD

1. Write to Farm Animals Reform Movement (FARM) and Food Animal Concerns Trust (FACT) for information on what's happening in the factory-farm movement.

2. Distribute their literature to schools and libraries in your town.

3. Arrange for a farm animal slide show in your school, civic club, or meeting of interested friends.

4. Consider your own eating habits. Discuss your concerns with your family and get their support.

5. Write to: U.S. Department of Agriculture
14th Street and Jefferson Drive, S.W.
Washington, D.C. 20250

and demand that antibiotics and other chemicals be eliminated from cattle feed. Perhaps you could get several of your friends to sign such a letter with you.

6. Vegetarianism is a personal matter. It is also a healthy way of life for millions of people, and certainly a positive step against factory farming. It may be something you'd like to know more about. If so, you can write to the Vegetarian Information Service.

ANIMALS IN THE WILD

If you think wild animals should be protected from hunters and trappers, you can do something about it. You can write to two congressional committees. They are looking into the situation that affects wild horses and burros. You might also mention your concern for all animals in the wild.

1. Energy and Natural Resources Committee
   United States Senate
   Washington, D.C. 20510
2. Committee on Interior and Insular Affairs
   United States House of Representatives
   Washington, D.C. 20510

If you would like to stop the use of the steel-jaw trap which kills and injures thousands of animals each year, you might write to:

California Children and Youth Against the Steel-Jaw Trap
c/o HSUS
1713 J Street, Suite 305
Sacramento, California 95814

If you are not from California but would like to know how to start a similar group in your state, write to them for petitions, information on how to write to assemblymen, and school information packets.

ANIMALS FOR RESEARCH

When you think of animals being used for research, you probably picture monkeys, cats, dogs, and pigs in some faraway laboratory. One of the ways you can help change this situation is to continue to write to your congressmen protesting the tragic waste and suffering of innocent animals.

As students, however, you may be able to do even more good by starting in your own school. Research animals are closer than you may realize. Many young science students are faced with animal experiments as early as junior high. What is happening in the schools in your community in this regard?

"No single experiment in high school or college advances human knowledge in the slightest," claims George K. Russell, associate professor of biology at Adelphi University in New York.

In an article for the *American Biology Teacher*, reprinted by SAR, Professor Russell continued by saying that, "In actual fact these studies are not experiments at all; they are simply demonstrations."

He feels that young people need to be inwardly connected to what they are learning about, as well as intellectually connected. In other words, they need to be given the opportunity to feel as well as think during the learning process.

Vivisection in the school laboratory, claims Professor Russell, does nothing to foster the natural affection that human beings have for animals. In fact, he feels it does just the opposite. Dissecting a frog, or a worm, or a cat actually severs or breaks the relationship that is there naturally.

In order to fulfill the assignment, many students try to "harden" themselves so they will not feel the pain of experimenting with or dissecting a fellow creature. Others get sick and stumble out of the room. Still others become detached and "scientific" and develop the attitude that the process is necessary for learning.

School counselor Gwen Hutchinson had something to say about this very topic—attitude. "In my work with students from fourth grade through high school," she said, "I see that we've almost ruled out the education of the heart in most classrooms by telling students what they can and cannot do." Animals are usually not even allowed in the classroom except in the science labs. And the purpose there is anything but humane.

"My father taught me to say 'No,' " added Gwen. "In fact, I'll never forget the time I was in ninth grade and my teacher told me to dissect a worm. I said, 'No,' and then after much arguing I left the room weeping."

The boys in the class chased and teased Gwen, running after her with their wiggly worms. But it didn't matter. "I didn't fail the class," added Gwen with a smile. "The important thing is that I did what was in my heart."

Whether or not to participate in animal experiments is a personal decision. But it is important enough for each person to consider seriously. As a young student, Gwen Hutchinson felt strongly enough about it that she said "No," risked being teased, and got in an argument with her teacher. But doing what her heart told her was right made her a stronger person.

College student Laura Simon also spoke out for what she knew was right. And she had the courage to do more than simply separate the injured mice. She went to the teachers themselves and the school newspaper where the possibility for some real changes could begin.

Thousands of other students in high schools and colleges around the United States are also speaking out for animals. As a result, the Student Action Corp for Animals (SACA) was formed in 1981 by a group of educators and community leaders, all active in the Animal Rights Movement. According to Director Rosa Feldman, "SACA is a grass roots organization," and its purpose is to encourage interested youth to "put their energy and concern to use in real ways that can help animals."

If you would like to find out more about SACA and/or become a member, write to the organization (address at the back of the book) and ask for their Student Action Pac for high school and college students. One of the group's primary goals at this time is to abolish dissection in school laboratories. Information about SACA's Stop Dissection Campaign is also available from the Washington, D.C., headquarters.

If you are looking for the best way you can contribute to the end of laboratory violence, whether in the research labs of a medical school or those in our junior and senior high schools, perhaps the first place to look is within your own heart. What, in your opinion needs to happen, and how can you help to bring it about?

"REVERENCE FOR ALL LIFE"

There is much work to be done. You may wonder if it's really worth it. What good will it do anyway? I'm just one person. I'm a kid. What can I possibly do to make a difference, you may ask.

You may also run into people who ask why you give time to defending the rights of animals when there is still so much human suffering in the world? "Aren't people more important than animals?" they may ask.

These are not easy questions to answer. I face them each day myself. As I see it, however, the issue of animal rights is not only a matter of treating animals humanely. It is also a matter of developing sensitive, caring human beings. And it is not a matter of choosing between animal life and human life. It is as Albert Schweitzer put it, a matter of developing a "reverence for all life."

I know in my own experience that whenever I stand on the side of life—whatever form it takes—I am a better person. I become more humane toward myself and others. And I am reminded of who I really am.

Perhaps that is where the real work needs to begin. We must start by recognizing life as a gift from our Creator, and ourselves as caretakers. As such, life is not ours to give or to take.

And it just may be that unless and until we are willing to share that gift with all creatures, we prevent the world from being the kingdom it really is.

APPENDIX
In Support of Animal Rights: National Organizations and Their Work

Following are some of the national associations and groups mentioned in this book that work in defense of animals. You may want to write to them for more information. You can also check with your librarian for the names and addresses of local chapters and groups that would welcome your support and participation.

American Horse Protection Association (AHPA)
   1904 T Street, N.W., Apt. A
   Washington, D.C. 20009
   The only national organization dedicated to the welfare of wild and domestic animals. Investigates and protests abuses of all horses. Publishes a newsletter. Has a junior division.
American Fund for Alternatives to Animal Research (AFAAR)
   175 West 12th Street, Suite 16G
   New York, New York 10011
   Provides grants to support biomedical research that does not use animals. Urges the ending of all such experiments. Publishes newsletter.

American Humane Association (AHA)

    5351 S. Roslyn Street

    Englewood, Colorado 80111

    Seeks to prevent cruelty to children and animals. Hollywood office provides consulting and supervisory service for animal action in films and television. Various publications.

American Society for the Prevention of Cruelty to Animals (ASPCA)

    441 E. 92nd Street

    New York, New York 10028

    Enforces laws for the protection of all animals. Promotes kindness and appreciation of animals. Investigates cruelty cases. Provides shelters and hospitals. Publishes wide variety of information on national humane issues.

Animal Care & Education Center (ACEC)

    P.O. Box 64

    Rancho Santa Fe, California 92067

    Nationally recognized nonprofit organization dedicated to improving human/animal relationships through a comprehensive public education program. Adoption program. Emergency treatment for wildlife. Publishes quarterly journal.

Animal Liberation (AL)

    319 W. 74th Street

    New York, New York 10023

    Vegetarians opposed to all animal experimentation involving pain or killing. Promotes welfare of all animals. Seeks to educate the public to the benefits of a vegetarian diet. Quarterly publication.

Animal Protection Institute of America (API)

    P.O. Box 22505

    Sacramento, California 95822

    Conducts educational, informational, and research programs to promote humane treatment of all animals, particularly pets, livestock, sea animals, and wildlife. Publishes quarterly magazine and various pamphlets and brochures.

Animal Rights Network (ARN)

P.O. Box 5234

Westport, Connecticut 06881

Seeks to promote greater communication and cooperation within the animal welfare/rights/liberation movement. Provides a forum in which people and groups can exchange ideas and discuss current animal-related issues. Publishes *Agenda*, the essential magazine of the movement, bimonthly.

Animal Welfare Institute (AWI)

P.O. Box 3650

Washington, D.C. 20007

Promotes humane treatment of animals, particularly those used in research and medicine. Publishes books and quarterly report.

Beauty Without Cruelty (BWC)

175 W. 12th Street

New York, New York 10011

Opposes the use of animals in the production of clothing and cosmetics. Educates public about the suffering of animals used for these purposes. Publishes newsletter and other reports.

Defenders of Wildlife (DOW)

1244 19th Street, N.W.

Washington, D.C. 20036

Educational group promoting wildlife protection. Publishes bimonthly magazine. Special division for young people.

Farm Animal Reform Movement (FARM)

P.O. Box 70123

Washington, D.C. 20088

National educational organization dedicated to alleviating and eliminating abuse and other problems of animal agriculture. Publishes newsletter and various brochures.

Food Animal Concerns Trust (FACT)

P.O. Box 14599

Chicago, Illinois 60614

Free information service for public interest organizations concerned with food, conservation, and animal protection. Newsletter and photographs available.

Friends of Animals (FOA)

11 W. 60th Street

New York, New York 10023

Works to reduce the number of stray animals. Offers low-cost spay/neuter programs. Also active against use of steel-jaw trap, wildlife abuse, and commercial furs. Publishes newsletter and bulletins. Welcomes young adult members.

Fund for Animals (FA)

140 W. 57th Street

New York, New York 10019

Works to protect wildlife and fight cruelty to domestic and wild animals. Publicizes and influences public opinion on animal issues. Publishes newsletter.

Humane Society of the United States (HSUS)

2100 L. Street, N.W.

Washington, D.C. 20037

Promotes humane treatment of animals and compassion in people. Educational division and youth division. Publishes quarterly magazine for adults and news magazine for young children.

The Institute for the Study of Animal Problems (ISAP)

2100 L. Street, N.W.

Washington, D.C. 20037

Research division of the HSUS. Uses scientific methods to study and investigate animal welfare issues. Publishes bi-monthly journal.

International Primate Protection League (IPPI)
P.O. Drawer X
Summerville, South Carolina 29483
Works to preserve and protect nonhuman primates in the wild and in nonhabitat countries. Seeks to improve conditions for primates in zoos and laboratories. Publishes quarterly newsletter and special project reports.

Mobilization for Animals (MFA)
P.O. Box 56272
Washington, D.C. 20011
Coalition of thirty-one organizations dedicated to protesting the use of animals in research. Members distribute literature, testify at legislative hearings, and plan and carry out demonstrations.

National Antivivisection Society (NAVS)
100 East Ohio Street
Chicago, Illinois 60611
Conducts programs and publishes materials to educate public on the evils of vivisection on animals. Publicizes and teaches the methods and means to combat it. Bimonthly bulletin, booklets, pamphlets, and other materials.

National Association for the Advancement of Humane Education (NAAHE)
P.O. Box 362
East Haddam, Connecticut 06423
Educational division of HSUS. Seeks to improve humane education programs nationally by providing leadership, practical ideas, and useful materials. Publishes quarterly magazine and newsletter, curriculum guide, and special reports.

People for the Ethical Treatment of Animals (PETA)
1710 Connecticut Avenue. N.W.
Washington, D.C. 20009
Works with Animal Rights Network and other activist

groups in an attempt to connect the wide range of animal rights' crusaders. Young, articulate, and dedicated members. Strong support on college campuses.

Society for Animal Rights (SAR)

421 S. State Street

Clarks Summit, Pennsylvania 18411

Organization whose main goal is to end the use of all animals in research. Publishes newsletter, books, pamphlets, and legal materials to alert people to the suffering of animals in all areas.

Student Action Corp for Animals (SACA)

423 Fifth Street, S.E.

Washington, D.C. 20003

United Action for Animals (UAA)

205 E. 42nd Street

New York, New York 10017

Promotes the use of modern, sophisticated research methods in place of live animals. Seeks laws to provide government funding of alternative methods. Publishes quarterly report.

Vegetarian Information Service (VIS)

P.O. Box 5888

Washington, D.C. 20014

Promotes health and nutritional benefits of vegetarian way of life. News of vegetarian movement. Publishes newsletter and leaflets.

Bibliography

Curtis, Patricia. *Animal Rights: Stories of People Who Defend the Rights of Animals.* New York: Four Winds Press, 1980.

Mason, Jim and Peter Singer. *Animal Factories.* New York: Crown Publishers, Inc., 1980.

McCoy, Joseph. *In Defense of Animals.* New York: Seabury Press, 1978.

Reusch, Hans. *Slaughter of the Innocent.* New York: Bantam Books, 1978.

Salt, Henry, *Animals' Rights.* Clarks Summit, Pennsylvania: Society for Animal Rights, 1980. Originally published in 1893.

Singer, Peter. *Animal Liberation: A New Ethics for our Treatment of Animals.* New York: Avon Books, 1975.

Magazines, newspapers, clippings, and various printed data from a vast variety of animal welfare organizations.

Index

141

California Children and Youth Against the Steel-Jaw Trap, 130
Calves. *See* Cattle
Capture of Grizzly Adams, The (film), 39
Cardboard, used in feed, 67-68
Cardiology program, computerized, 110-112
Cat People (film), 41
Cats, 10-11, 12, 21, 22, 27, 30-33, 35, 37, 45, 55, 88-89, 130, 131
Cattle, 12, 14, 15, 17, 48, 49-50, 51, 54, 60-63, 67, 69
Celebrities, vegetarian, 71-72
Cell cultures, research and, 115-116
Chemicals, 67, 69, 115, 118, 119, 120, 129
Chickens, 53-54, 55-58, 67
"Chisholms, The," 15, 39-40
Coalition to Stop Draize and LD-50, 117
Cockfights, 39, 51
Committee on Interior and Insular Affairs, U. S. House of Representatives, 130
Compassionate Shopper, The, 127
Computers, use of, as research alternative, 110-112
Confinement, raising animals in, 53-68
Cows. *See* Cattle
Coyotes, 69, 77, 88, 89
Creator, 13, 133
Cultures, cell. *See* Cell cultures

Daredevil/reality programs, 41-42
Deer, 75, 77, 81, 88, 129
Defenders of Wildlife, 136
De Groot, Alice, 23
"Discovery of Animal Behavior, The," 42
Dissection in school laboratories, 132
Dog races, 51, 128
Dogs, 9, 12, 14, 17, 18, 19, 21, 22, 27, 28-30, 31, 33-34, 35, 37, 55, 64, 88, 89, 90, 98, 99, 100-101, 105, 130
Draize test, 94
  replacement for, 116-117
Drugs, 69, 119
  anticancer, 119
Ducks, 15, 40, 58, 77

Eagles, 77, 81, 88
Educational programs, 22-28, 30, 31, 37-38, 47, 51-52, 72, 88, 126, 128
Elephants, 15, 44
Elliott, Sir William, 66-67

Endangered species, 44, 45, 46, 47, 74-89
Endangered Species Act, 79
Energy and Natural Resources Committee, U. S. Senate, 130
Entertainment, and exploitation of animals, 15-16, 39-52
Euthanasia, 9, 21, 37, 98, 100, 103

Factory farming, 14, 53-73, 129
Farm Animal Reform Movement, 125, 129, 136-137
Federal Drug Administration, 69, 94
Films, exploitation of animals for, 15-16, 39-42, 51, 128
Fish and Wildlife Service, U. S., 78-79
Flank strap, 49
Food Animal Concerns Trust, 55, 129, 137
Fox, 81, 87, 88
Fox, Dr. Michael, 18
Friends of Animals, 137
Friends of Cats (San Diego), 33
Frogs, 131
Fund for Animals, 29, 137

George Whittell Wildlife Rehabilitation Center, 84-85
Goats, 47, 77
Golakoff, Ivan, 24-27, 45-46
Grandin, Temple, 66
Gregory, Dick, 65
Guide Dogs for the Blind, 122

Hall, Martha, 81-89
Hardin County (Ohio) dog pound, 9
Hawks, 81, 87
Heaven's Gate (film), 16
Hinchee, Ray, 75
Hogs. *See* Pigs
Horse racing, 51, 128
Horseback riding, therapeutic, 25, 26
Horses, 10, 11, 15-16, 17, 25, 26, 34, 39, 40-41, 48-49, 51, 69, 82
  wild, 76, 77, 79-81, 130
Humane Education (magazine), 127
Humane screening techniques, 119
Humane Society (Lackawanna County, Pennsylvania), 22
Humane Society of the United States, 10, 28, 48, 77, 79, 122, 127, 128, 137
Hutchinson, George, 31, 35, 36
Hutchinson, Gwen, 31, 35-38, 42, 45, 72-73, 131-132

142

143

144